Life isn't just a

PANIC

Stories of Hope by Recovering Agoraphobics

edited by Anita L. Pace

Baby Steps Press

Beaverton, Oregon 97075

Published in the United States by
Baby Steps Press
P.O. Box 1917
Beaverton, OR 97075

First Edition, First Printing

Cover art: Lauren Dye,
Moon Madness Production, Portland, OR

Typesetting: Lauren Dye and
Barbara Whitaker Computer Services

Illustrations by Nancy DeLouise

Tree illustration by Harriet F. Carpenter

"No More One of the Walking, Wounded, Living Dead" by Dr. Marilyn Gellis, reprinted with permission by Dr. Gellis from her book, "From Anxiety Addict to Serenity Seeker," 1990.

"Journey," by Anita L. Pace, originally appeared in "Echoes from the Heart, An Anthology of Women's Poetry," Volume 1, 1982.

"What to Do If a Family Member Has an Anxiety Disorder" printed with permission by Sally Winston, Psy. D., The Anxi-ety and Stress Disorders Institute of Maryland, Towson, MD, 1992.

"Strategies for Coping with Panic" printed with permission by Jerilyn Ross, M.A., L.I.C.S.W., The Ross Center for Anxiety and Related Disorders, Inc., Washington DC Adapted from Mathews **et al.**, 1981.

ISBN: 0-9631666-3-8

Library of Congress Catalog Card Number: 95-94246

Printed In the United States by McNaughton & Gunn

"No one is braver than an agoraphobic on their road to recovery. Panic and Agoraphobia rob the life of the people who suffer from them. These are stories of courage and by people just like you who have taken the steps necessary to recapture their lives and not only survive but also triumph over their anxieties. My congratulations to all who have resisted the temptation to hide forever in that 'safe place' and instead faced the fear of the unknown and found their peace beyond."

Charles R. Cobb, M.D.
Panic, Anxiety & Phobic Disorders
Treatment Program of Northeastern Oklahoma

"Anita Pace's *Life Isn't Just a Panic* is a collection of writings of people who have suffered from, struggled with, and shown great courage in their attempts to overcome Panic Disorder and Agoraphobia. People currently suffering with these disorders will easily identify with the stories contained in this book and will no longer feel alone in their struggles. The reader will note a common thread running throughout this book; with courage, determination, and persistent direct confrontation of their fears, most people reap the rewards of significant improvement. Fortunately, appropriate medications and cognitive behavior therapy now offer great hope to the majority of people with Panic Disorder and Agoraphobia."

Ricks Warren, Ph.D.
Director, The Anxiety Disorders Clinic
Lake Oswego, OR

"*Life Isn't Just a Panic* contains true stories that inspire, and even more important, inform with ideas about how to manage and overcome the symptoms of agoraphobia and panic disorder in order to live a productive and satisfying life."

Shirley Devol VanLieu, Ph.D.

"*Life Isn't Just a Panic* presents a blend of first-person stories, humorous illustrations, facts from the National Institute of Mental Health, and resources for anxiety sufferers. The first-person stories capture the struggle that many patients with anxiety disorders encounter with themselves, their symptoms, family members, and the health care system. This book may be a valuable resource for both consumers and the professionals caring for them."

Manuel E. Tancer, M.D.
Assoc. Professor of Psychiatry and Behavioral Neurosciences
Wayne State University School of Medicine
Director of Psychiatry Research
Veterans Administration Medical Center

To those in my life
who never questioned me
when I said, "I can't right now,"
and supported me so that now I often
"can."
Thank you for believing me
and believing in me.

Acknowledgements

This project began with an idea and continued with support and encouragement from many. My thanks to much help from Lynn Cave of the National Institute of Mental Health who provided me with much information to help me get the word out about the needed stories and gave me lots of information directly. Thanks to Mary Guardino, Shirley Green, Cyma Siegal Pat Merrill, Franci Warner and Charles Cobb, M.D. for running my call for submissions in their newsletters. Thanks to Dr. Marilyn Gellis and Carolyn Dickman for time and support. Thanks to Caree Vander Linden from the National Institute of Mental Health who helped me in my search for doctors to review this book. Thanks to Ronald Doctor, Ph.D. for writing the Foreword, to Drs. Charles R. Cobb, Stan Gurman, William D. Kernodle, Manuel E. Tancer, and to Michele Carter, Ph.D., Shirley VanLieu, Ph.D., and Ricks Warren, Ph.D. for taking the time to review this book and offer much moral support. Thanks to Jerilyn Ross, M.A.,L.I.C.S.W. and Sally Winston, Psy.D. for giving permission to reprint information they've written. Thanks to Maggie Schie-Lurie from the National Alliance for the Mentally Ill for providing me with information. Thanks to Sharon Castlen for support in many areas regarding publication and distribution. Thanks to Lauren Dye, Barb Whitaker, and Nancy DeLouise for book production assistance. Thanks to Harriet Carpenter for help in many ways, especially for your financial assistance for this project. A special thank you to Susan Turner for assisting me in so many ways: editing, providing vital information, typing, offering opinions, and giving me moral support through many tough days. And, of course, to all the courageous contributors who shared their stories, a special thank you, too. Without your willingness to come forth and speak out, there'd be no book for others to gain from.

Foreword

We know that mythology is an expression of the universal aspects of human experience that reside deep within each of us because of our connection with the human life stream. They tell us of what could be; things that we don't always see from our vantage point within. Anita Pace's wonderful book, *Life Isn't Just a Panic; Stories of Hope by Recovering Agoraphobics*, touch any of us who have had to confront and overcome adversity in our lives. It is particularly relevant and inspiring to those of us who have had panic attacks and/or agoraphobia because it offers, not only a shared understanding of these experiences, but also stories of recovery and renewal.

One of the most dreaded creatures in human mythology is the dragon. In western tradition, there are many mythological stories about the dragon who generally lives in a cave and appears when least expected, much as panic attacks seem to come "out of the blue." The dragon is fierce and horribly frightening in size, power, and tenacity. Dragons breath fire and represent an image of an immense obstacle. For those of us who have experienced panic attacks, the dragon is a physical form that epitomizes the dread, helplessness, horror, and pain that one experiences in the panic attack. For those who stay to face the dragon or who come back to face the dragon, they begin to learn that the dragon is the guardian of a great treasure hidden in the cave. The dragon itself doesn't always know the value of the treasure; it is unconscious, but has dedicated itself to guarding it tenaciously.

The stories you are about to read have to do more with discovery of the treasure than with the dragon. The dragon must be faced, but for what reason? If there is only a dragon, then most people would choose to just have nothing to do with it. They'd avoid it. To decide to face it means that you want the treasure and are willing to deal with the dragon in order to have it. But what is the treasure? The treasure is in essentially finding yourself and freeing yourself from the dragons within; facing issues of separation so you can establish or find your identity ... facing negative, unacceptable emotions, such as anger, and integrating that energy into your life ... facing social fears so you can have self-esteem, identity, and intimacy, facing the impossible so that you can be free of dependency on others and take your place as an individual... facing death of your physical being and death of the unconscious dragons within that hide the treasure of your unique and loving being. And all the while there is "hope" or a faith that that treasure is really there behind the fearsome dragon.

Just as myth conveys human truths, these stories convey truth about the process of recovery from panic and agoraphobia, the courage to face these fears and the treasure that is available to each of us who undertake this process.

Ron Doctor, Ph.D.

Founding Board Member of the
Anxiety Disorders Association of America

Professor of Psychology,
California State University, Northridge

Table of Contents

Important Note

Many authors in this book have written of their experiences, positive and negative, with various medications. Remember this is their experience. Please **do not** use any medications for the treatment of panic attacks or agoraphobia without the prescription of, and the supervision by, a licensed medical professional.

Also, the use of any medications or treatment programs written of in *Life Isn't Just a Panic; Stories of Hope by Recovering Agoraphobics* is neither endorsed nor condemned by Baby Steps Press or Anita L. Pace.

Introduction

I was 13 years old in an eighth grade math class when I first experienced a panic attack. From then and through college I endured hundreds of these terrifying episodes, not knowing what they were. Although I earned a BA in Social Welfare with plans to become a therapist, I never heard the term "Panic Disorder." I did read a couple of paragraphs about Agoraphobia in one of my classes, but I didn't recognize myself in the description of this strange illness.

By 26 I was on Disability, housebound and severely riddled with constant anxiety, even in the supposed safe confines of my apartment. It was then that I became most ill and believed I'd spend the rest of my life as I was; weak, unable to talk to people, hyperventilating for several hours at a time, and choking for no apparent reason. As many of the writers whose stories appear here have stated or implied, my life became Hell.

Recovery has been a full time job for some 18 years and will no doubt continue on. At my worst, getting off the sofa for a minute at a time to wash dishes was a big step. It was years later that the thought of writing a book on Panic Disorder and Agoraphobia tugged at me. At the same time, I feared it, not wanting to relive the anguish that I'd known every day for years. I also feared that concentrating on this subject would induce panic attacks with a fury.

I finally decided to not just write my story for a book, but to include the experiences of many. I asked several anxiety and panic-related newsletter editors to include my call for submissions in their publications. I wanted contributors to write their stories, but I wanted them to share therapies, techniques, methods, and little tricks that have helped them recover that might help others. I didn't discourage these authors from writing of their horror or feelings of hopelessness. Including stories of those who used to feel such desperation and are now recovering could make a dramatic impact on readers who feel hopeless now.

From the press releases and by word of mouth, I acquired the stories and poems contained in this book. Submissions came from across the United States, from the West to East coasts, from Northern states, through Middle America, and from the South. There were women and men who responded, as young as 18 and up to the late 50's or early 60's as far as I know. Stories came from those in large cities and small ones, too. Different backgrounds, different cultures, different people, but the same in many ways.

This sampling of people cannot speak for all who have ever suffered from anxiety disorders. No two situations are exactly alike, but the desire here is to present stories that give hope and make the reader feel less alone. A goal, too, is to give more information and educate those who are learning about such disorders, as well as those who treat them.

There were a few themes that reappeared. One was that many of the authors have felt frustrated with the help they've received at one time or another. Some wrote they have had wonderful therapists, but several have felt like guinea pigs and at times more knowledgeable of their condition than the professionals they were being treated by.

I was surprised by the number of contributors who had experienced deaths of loved ones and other major stresses about the time that their attacks began. Many began having severe anxiety while adults, but there were those who began experiencing these disorders in school at a young age.

When I created Baby Steps Press in 1990, it was for the purpose of publishing one anthology, Write from the Heart, Lesbians Healing from Heartache. But the next year I wrote a growing up story entitled If You Want to Soar, You've Got to Learn to Fly.

Life Isn't Just a Panic ; Stories of Hope by Recovering Agoraphobics is my third book, but Baby Steps Press wouldn't exist without the thousands of baby steps I've had to take to get to the point of being able to publish that first book. Being able to publish this book is a personal accomplishment especially close to my heart.

I've suffered as I imagine most of the readers have suffered. Whether it be from an anxiety disorder or any other life challenge, it is important to me that my books convey how much we beings have in common. There is so much pain in our lives at one time or another, and understanding the feelings of others is most important, I believe. On a personal level, I've been saddened and angered when people have not believed me when I've said I can't do something or another. Yes, most of us need a kick in the pants at times or else will sit on our duffs most our lives, procrastinating it away. Yet I've learned that many of us with anxiety disorders are often high-achievers and perfectionists, guilt-ridden for not accomplishing more in our lives. When lives are interrupted and affected by anxiety, it is not an indication that people with anxiety are lazy, trying to ignore responsibilities, or not wanting to be contributing members to their families, friends, and society. Too often these "invisible" disabilities have not been recognized for what they are by others, only adding to frustration in attempts to live productive lives. I want this book to demonstrate and educate about the difficulty of living with anxiety disorders and how much work and courage it takes to live each day. So increased understanding is another goal of this book.

The stories and poems on these pages represent but a sample of the millions of people who suffer from Panic Disorder and Agoraphobia, but we've shared the terror as one. I hope that the handful of stories here speak for many, giving consolation to those who have felt isolation, and encouragement to those who have felt discouragement and despair. If you have Panic Disorder, Agoraphobia, or any anxiety disorder, you are not alone. There is help and you can have a productive, satisfying, and full life.

Sincerely,

Anita L. Pace

"It takes an agoraphobic to understand an agoraphobic."

Rochelle Krupp
from her contribution,
The Pain Hidden Deep Inside

What is Panic Disorder?

In panic disorder, brief episodes of intense fear are accompanied by multiple physical symptoms (such as heart palpitations and dizziness) that occur repeatedly and unexpectedly in the absence of any external threat. These "panic attacks," which are the hallmark of panic disorder, are believed to occur when the brain's normal mechanism for reacting to a threat - the "fight or flight" response - becomes aroused for no apparent reason.

Panic attacks typically occur spontaneously, with no apparent trigger. They can even occur during sleep. Though they usually last for a few minutes, they can feel like an eternity.

Information provided by the National Institute of Mental Health (NIMH) booklet "Understanding Panic Disorder"

What is Agoraphobia?

Those with panic disorder sometimes become afraid of any place or situation where escape might be difficult or help unavailable in case of a panic attack. Because of fears about situations that they associate with panic disorder, they may have chronic fear. Normal everyday activities like grocery shopping, traveling, and leaving home may become greatly restricted. This condition is called agoraphobia. It affects about a third of all people with panic disorder.

Typically, people with agoraphobia fear being in crowds, standing in line, entering shopping malls, and riding in cars or public transportation. These people often restrict themselves to a "zone of safety" that may include only the home or the immediate neighborhood. Any movement beyond the edges of this zone creates mounting anxiety. Sometimes a person with agoraphobia is unable to leave the home alone, but can travel if accompanied by a particular family member or friend.

People with agoraphobia can be seriously disabled by their condition. Some are unable to work, and they may need to rely heavily on other family members who must do the shopping and run all the errands, as well as accompany the affected person on rare excursions outside the "safety zone." The person with agoraphobia, then, typically leads a life of extreme dependency as well as great discomfort.

Information provided by the National Institute of Mental Health (NIMH) booklet "Understanding Panic Disorder"

If I Cried
by Brenda E. Eads

If I cried, it would be for
songs I didn't sing
When I wanted to

If I cried, it would be for
words of comfort I didn't say
When I needed to

If I cried, it would be for
actions that were stillborn
When I tried to

If I cried, it would be for
this illness has made me selfish
Always thinking first

How will this affect me
When sometimes
I am only a minor player

But I think

It is not all bad to
consider myself first
for awhile

Now that I have

And found myself not unlovely
I want to not be
this way any longer

Maybe I would still cry

But how much better
to cry over acts committed
than those omitted

Because of fear.

Greetings From a Survivor of Hell
by Susan Turner

I have been a resident in a place called Hell and have clawed my way back up. No, I have not risen from the dead, although at times I truly thought or wished I had died. Hell to me is ... SEVERE AGORAPHOBIA!

I'm the oldest of four children. My childhood was fairly normal, I thought, until I looked back on it as an adult. My daddy was a loud, gentle, friendly, outrageously funny man. He suffered from many addictions and later in life was diagnosed with manic-depression.

My mother was the super strict disciplinarian of our family. I perceived that she loved me conditionally, so for many years I strived to please her ... that is until reaching adolescence in the 60's. She later became my biggest cheerleader and loving support system. As a child and teenager, I didn't really fit the agoraphobic profile. I was not an overachiever or perfectionist. That came later.

In 1987, I was married with two sons who I basically raised on my own. My husband worked out of town a lot, coming home only on weekends. I worked at an elementary school as a teacher's assistant, attended college, volunteered at the YMCA, and ran my kids all over creation. I was overwhelmed and overstressed ... it's not easy being perfect! I had become the extreme perfectionist and overachiever, thinking that I WAS MY ACCOMPLISHMENTS. I was everything to everybody and definitely headed for a crash.

April 23, 1987 is a day etched in my mind forever. This is when my descent into Hell began. It was a Wednesday and a very hot day. I was supervising kids drawing with chalk on the blacktop, bending up and down a lot. I suddenly felt dizzy, sweaty, and saw spots before my eyes. These sensations scared the hell out of me. I rushed into the classroom, not knowing what else to do, only to be asked by my teacher why I wasn't outside. Embarrassed and not knowing what to say, I tried to go out the door that led to the blacktop. But as soon as I stepped outside, I was bombarded with those scary feelings again. I was so afraid that all I could think of was getting back inside where I felt better.

Not knowing how to explain what was happening to my teacher, I literally finished my shift with one foot in the room and one foot out. When I left school, I felt better, so I decided to go to our local mall. But as I entered the mall, I froze; the bodily sensations returned! I drove home as fast as I could and fell on the couch. While I pondered what had just happened, I chalked it up to not eating and to the heat. I managed to run some errands later on that day, but was very apprehensive that those weird feelings would return. They didn't. When I entered school the next day, I was a bit shaky, but I got through my shift.

Friday, April 25th was the clincher! Ten minutes into the school day, my teacher called me to the front of the class. I got halfway there when I was overwhelmed with the feeling that the room was spinning around me. I was hot and cold, my whole body was tingling, and the world seemed to go black. Mumbling something to the teacher, I ran to the nurse's office. Once there, I couldn't lay down or stand still. All I knew was I had to get home fast! I couldn't even go back to the class for my purse. A friend that happened to be in the hall had to retrieve it for me. With purse in hand, I broke all records getting home. As I lay on the couch, I knew something was terribly wrong with me. A few hours later, I began to feel calmer, so I thought I'd attempt to run some last minute Easter errands.

I tried to open the car door three times. Each time the frightening body symptoms enveloped me and I ran back to my house. Finally, I jumped in my car and "white-knuckled" it. I don't remember doing my errands, but they got done.

The next day I went to one of those open- most- of- the - time medical clinics. Listening to my horror story and checking me, the woman doctor diagnosed me with panic disorder. At that time I didn't know what a rarity it was to be diagnosed correctly on the first try. Unfortunately, just having a name for my condition didn't make me feel much better. She suggested that I see a psychiatrist. When I told her I didn't know any, she handed me a list. I picked the closest one (shades of things to come?) and made an appointment to see the doctor the following Monday.

I took the day off from school and "anxiously" waited for my appointment. I tried to drive myself there, but I freaked out, so I turned around and had my husband drive me. When I explained to the doctor what had been going on with me, he handed me the anti-panic medication Xanax, and I swallowed it on the spot. It seemed to calm me down a bit. We talked our 50 minute hour, he wrote me a prescription for Xanax, and we made another appointment.

I'm panicking everywhere. All I want to do is run home where I feel safe. I try to enter a store that I've shopped at for years and the store seems as if it's spinning around me. My eyes get blurry or I see a brilliant white glow. I feel like I'm not real and my entire body feels like a tightly wound spring. I break out in a cold sweat and my mind fills up with panicky frantic thoughts. I leave shopping carts in the middle of aisles and head home when a block from my destination, totally unable to drive one foot further.

With my life falling apart, being perfect didn't seem that important anymore. I dropped out of college even though I had the highest grades in my classes. I stopped working at the YMCA, stopped grocery shopping, banking, and everything else that most people can do easily. I finished out the school year at my job by making several modifications; my husband had to drive my car and leave it there (in case I had to escape). He had to walk home. My husband took over most of my "out in the world" responsibilities or came with me. I saw my psychiatrist twice a week doing "talk therapy" and taking Xanax, but I kept getting worse instead of better.

I think he knew I needed a different kind of therapy because he offered to pay for the TERRAP tape program. Knowing how my husband felt about that "kind of help," I declined. I had anxiety all the time, so I didn't feel comfortable anywhere, although I did feel the least anxiety in my house. My life was spinning out of control and my world became smaller and smaller.

Avoidance became my middle name and agoraphobia invaded my life.

When the middle of June arrived and I didn't have to push myself out into the world, I didn't, except for my weekly visits to my therapist with my husband driving. But when my psychiatrist went on vacation the first of July, that was it.

I'm completely homebound. I can't even go out to my mailbox without panicking. This has marked my arrival in Hell! I'm having attacks in my house which had once been my only sanctuary. There's only a few rooms I feel any safety in. I even have to make dinner standing by a chair for support.

I decided that Xanax was making me worse, so I talked to my psychiatrist into giving me Valium, even though I knew it wasn't an anti-panic medication. I'd taken it in the past for nervousness, so I felt safe with it. But I'd developed a medicine phobia, so I took bits and pieces of the Valium. The life I'd once led and the person I once was were gone. In their place was left a self-imposed prison and a person racked with fear, who for most of the day only felt some relief laying on the couch or bed.

Besides the crippling panic and desperate depression I felt, I also dealt with agonizing guilt. My husband worked out of town all week only to come home to a wife who could no longer do anything out of the house. He had to do all my outside chores.

I felt guilty about my sons, Jace and Johnny. Where was the mother who only the summer before was able to take them anywhere they wanted to go wile their summer vacation? That mother was gone. In her place was left an anxious, depressed, and distracted person who couldn't walk out the front door. My husband coped the best he could and didn't complain very much. (He's the kind of man who just accepts things as they come and rises to the occasion).

Jace, who was going to enter the eighth grade in the fall, was another story. We didn't have a great relationship to begin with, and this was the last thing it needed. I could see the look of anger, confusion, and disgust in his eyes, so I never asked him for help. His reaction to my problem was to detach from me.

My younger son, Johnny, starting the sixth grade, accepted how I had changed. It bothered him to have to ask a friend's mother to take him places. One day we were talking about it when I asked him what he said to his friend. Nonchalantly, he said, "I told Todd you went crazy!" I wasn't sure how I felt about that answer, because I knew I wasn't crazy.

The very worst thing that an agoraphobic mother could experience has happened. Johnny went to the beach with a friend and his mother. I got a phone call that he fell down a fifty foot cliff and is being rushed to a hospital no more than three miles away! A friend has offered to take me to the hospital, but I'm paralyzed! I CAN'T GO. All I can do is hang on to my friend, shaking and crying. My son is in a hospital about ten minutes from me, going through three brain scans and I'm not there to comfort him. If that's not residing in the bowels of Hell, what is?

As the summer progressed, I could barely speak on the phone because even that simple act made me feel trapped. Every time the phone rang, I jumped! I'd allow very few people to come over. I wouldn't even let my poor parents who lived four hours away visit me. They had to deal with their own confusion and guilt ... ("Did we do this to her?")

September was the pits. My sons went back to school and I should've gone with them. Instead, I sat in my house crying and filled with fear. A week after school began, a former co-worker called to see how I was doing. When I told her, she referred me to a therapist who specializes in panic disorder. Where was this person with this vital information months ago? If I'd had the proper treatment from the beginning, I believe I would've never developed agoraphobia.

I began working with Kathy, an MFCC. She became my guide through the maze of agoraphobia. She had to come to my house because I couldn't go to her. We've worked together for several years and some things she's said have been very important to me. At our first meeting she said, "We are starting from right now. We have to get you out of the house. Later, if you want, we can go back and work on your life stuff." She also told me that we have to find things out in the world that are important enough so that I'd risk feeling panicky ... "markets aren't going to get you out there!" She also said, "You are important and lovable just because you are on Earth. You don't have to achieve anything."

That's still hard for me to believe.

One of the first things Kathy had me do is listen to a progressive relaxation tape twice daily. I found that type of relaxation wasn't helpful for me, although many people have found it so. I prefer guided imagery tapes. Kathy also taught me diaphragmatic breathing techniques. They were difficult for me to master, but I've noticed proper breathing has helped me when I start experiencing some of the anxiety symptoms.

Kathy lets me complain about my latest symptom for a half hour. Then she literally pushes me out the door. We walk down my block one house at a time. Each step is pure terror, but I know that if I want my life back I have to do the hard work involved. I practice walking by myself the other days ... one step at a time. I finally made it to the end of my block. I'm excited and frightened at the same time; excited because I achieved my first big goal, and frightened because I can't see my house! I feel this wonderful sense of freedom I haven't felt in months.

Kathy has started taking me out in her car. This is not a pleasant experience. I've been returning home with my fingernails dug into my palms. I'm reading every book I can find on panic attacks and agoraphobia. I take something from each book that I think is appropriate for me. My favorite book is Don't Panic, by Reid Wilson. It makes a lot of sense to me. I saw Marianne Williamson on Oprah, talking about a book she wrote. I thought she was so interesting, that I bought the book on tape and started listening to it as I drove. I immediately realized that listening to books on tape is a great tool with driving because it diverts my attention away from bodily symptoms.

I've had a frightening realization; not even Kathy, who I once considered my savior, can stop me from suffering a major panic attack. But it's made me learn that safety comes from within. This feels like the beginning of my ascent up from Hell.

I breathe correctly, saying positive things to myself. I'm getting back into the world, but it's such a slow process. I get frustrated at times because I can't understand why it has taken me only a few months to become homebound while recovery seems to be taking forever. Depression ebbs and flows. Occasionally, I'm plagued with suicidal thoughts that started during the summer. Sometimes on my walks, I consider wandering into the path of an oncoming car, but as depressed as I am, I can't leave that legacy to my family.

My boundaries expanded slowly but surely. This is not to say it was easy. I'd go into stores I'd practiced in for days that I'd feel fairly comfortable in, then panic. Walking down the block was still hard sometimes, and on occasion I had to turn my car around and head home. But I persevered. I saw two options; 1) Continuing to fight my way back into the world, or 2) Returning to my house never to be seen again.

In March of 1988, Kathy suggested trying Xanax again because she believed it could help me in the stage of recovery I was in. Still a medicine phobic, I debated myself, then decided to go for it. I don't take enough to stop a panic attack, but it allows me to enter the world a little more comfortably.

June of 1988 was to be an exciting month for our family. Jace was graduating from Junior High School and Johnny from elementary. I wanted to try to attend both ceremonies, so I made these events my next big goals.

Getting to both schools presented me with two different obstacles. Jace's school was downtown ... way out of my comfort zone. The saving grace was that since I'd never been there, I had no scary memories attached to it. But Johnny was graduating from the school where I'd suffered my two major panic attacks the year before. Although only three minutes away, I dreaded returning there.

So Kathy and I worked on getting to both schools during our sessions. It took four sessions to get to Jace's school and walk into the auditorium. We practiced going to Johnny's school twice. My mother did graduation shopping for me, buying dresses for me to try on because I wasn't able to get to our malls as yet.

Kathy accompanied me to the graduations. I was able to stay and watch both ceremonies! Sitting in both auditoriums like any other parent was worth all the hard work and money I'd

spent to get there. I felt anxious the entire time, but the importance of what I was doing overrode my symptoms.

However, this was nothing compared to what I next had to
face. My daddy had been in and out of the hospital for a few years,
but being an extremely strong and resilient man, he always
managed to bounce back. Our family felt he prolonged his life
long enough to see my brother get married through sheer will
power. But on September 26, 1988, my daddy died. I was hysterical. He was one of the few people who I felt loved me unconditionally (I was his princess) and I felt gripped with tremendous
fear. How was I going to get to his funeral which would be held
four hours away? I called Kathy immediately.

I was surprised she could understand me through my
sobs. When she calmed me down, we discussed my options. After
much reflection, I knew that I couldn't make the trip. My mother
was very understanding. She said my daddy was no longer with
us and I should remember him as he was on his last visit; he was
no longer the gregarious father from my youth. He'd become
quiet and subdued. I recalled how we once sat on my porch and
shared two special hours together as I tried to explain to him what
was happening to me.

My husband and sons attended the funeral. Kathy and I
had our own memorial for my daddy at the exact time his was
being held more than two hundred miles away. At an old de-
serted baseball diamond, we looked through my family scrap
book. I shared my fond and loving memories of my daddy with
Kathy and buried a flower that I'd brought. I said my last good-
byes and was at peace with my decision because I felt his presence
there with me.

I don't have a strong faith in God, but I do in my daddy.
Although he died confused about my disorder and without
witnessing my full ascent, I believe he is looking down on me
from a far better place and is giving me his strength. For years I
had a photo of him in my car that I could look at when I began to
panic. My anxiety would lessen. Every night in bed I'd talk to him
and ask him to give me the courage to face another day. Out in the
world I could feel his hand in mine when I experienced my scary
symptoms and thought I was going to panic.

I KNOW he is always with me. His belief in me, from above, has a lot to do with my decision to keep moving forward. When I begin to falter or doubt, I know his spirit steps in to guide and protect me.

I'm using a tool called my Out in the World Book. It's a spiral notebook in which I chronicle all my outings. I write how I feel each day, where I go, how I feel. Besides aiding me in seeing patterns of behavior, it's fantastic to see how far I've come. I must have at least 20 books now. I found my first notebook and saw: "10:00 relaxation, 12:00 walk six houses, 2:00 relaxation, 4:00 walk seven houses." My feelings were bittersweet reading some of those first steps.

The strategy that's working best for me is getting out everyday and exposing myself to anxious situations. I go out armed with the knowledge that I have given myself PERMISSION to turn around at anytime. I try to change those What ifs around as soon as I think them. I use coping statements when my anxiety begins to rise. I stay in the present as much as possible and become involved with the world around me. And, of course, I use my "baby steps" in new situations. If I am going to a new place, I check it out ahead of time for parking, windows, doors, and bathrooms.

In 1990, I decided to start the only support group in my area. This was a giant leap of faith for me because of my fear of committing to do anything. I networked with many wonderful people and went through a basic counseling program. My motivation kept me going, despite the anxiety I felt.

Since 1992, I've been working with people dealing with panic disorder and agoraphobia. Today I can say I ACCEPT where I am in my recovery. This was not always the case. I fought against ACCEPTANCE.

I used to seek the magic pill or cure, although I know there isn't any. I'd hear about a new medication and call my psychiatrist. We'd discuss it and I'd either order it and not take it or just forget about it. I went through four tape programs, three of which were fairly good. But they only reinforced what I already knew. I've discovered there is no magic pill or cure ... there is just the hard work that no one else can do but me.

It's now been eight and a half years since my initial major panic attacks. I consider myself functioning, but with some limitations. That's okay. I know my work is not over yet and there are still goals to achieve. I deal with anxiety attacks almost daily, but now I can usually talk my way through them. Most importantly, I am now a resident of *this* world, even if my horrendous visit to Hell is not a too distant memory ... and one I will never forget.

The Art of Anxiety
by A. B.

I was born in 1940 in an area with cattails and marshlands near the ocean. The cattails bent in the winter winds.

Ours was a large extended family and there was much closeness. I had an older brother and a younger sister and was dependent on both. I was also the follower, observer, and worrier. My family lived with my paternal grandparents who were Sicilian. They had six daughters, each in a different stage of hysteria. I remember my grandmother looking out over the swamps, looking far beyond the new world, reaching back for Palermo. She hadn't wanted to come to the United States in the first place, and she was never allowed to return.

We moved to an apartment several miles away when I was three. My mother was Neapolitan and glad to move from her in-laws' house as the Sicilians seemed more depressed and worrisome than the Neapolitans.

The apartment was above a dress factory and the war was on. I felt frightened when we had to sit in the dark during Blackouts. We'd have to turn the lights off when the sirens blared. One time an Air Raid warden blew his whistle because we had a bathroom light on and he saw it through the fogged glass and our curtain. "You want the Gerrys to find us?!" he yelled.

We moved again in 1944 to a house my father bought with a big yard in a quiet neighborhood. I enjoyed living there and was very happy much of the time. One day I walked in the house and overheard my mother talking to a real estate person on the phone. They were selling the house. I went into a temper tantrum, lying on the floor, screaming. It was the shock of it. Nothing was ever discussed with us. They didn't want us to get upset.

The forties seemed to be the enema years. That wasn't discussed with us, either. My parents would start *the preparation* and speak in Italian at the first sign of trouble. We didn't know which one of us was the next victim, especially if all of us felt sick or looked a bit yellow. I didn't understand the logic. We were Sicilian. We all looked a bit yellow! We'd run and hide until they'd catch the one they wanted.

My father built a new home for us in 1949, only blocks from the old neighborhood, but it seemed far away. I rarely went back, but I missed my old home. The advantage of oil heat didn't compensate for the separation from everything I'd grown so fond of. I felt very alone.

My father built another house next door to this new one and we moved again within a year. I had several episodes of anxiety, feeling fear, but not panic.

And within a year, my father built yet another house next to the one we'd just moved into and we moved again.

In 1952, our family took a trip to Florida with my uncle and his wife and daughter. Being a close family also meant all eight of us drove down in one car. I sat on someone's lap from New York to Baltimore. When I stood up in Baltimore, I almost passed out. We arrived in St. Petersburg where my mother's parents were staying and rented a cottage for a week.

One day we went to the beach. I was sitting with my family when suddenly I got very confused and fearful. I ran to the car. I didn't understand what was happening to me and I felt very disoriented. This was my first anxiety attack.

In 1952 I dreaded the start of the eighth grade. Within a month of the school year, I had several panic attacks. I'd run out of school, fearing my mother wouldn't be home. I had separation anxiety when I was home and my parents weren't, as well as when I went to school and knew my parents would be leaving the house.

I felt embarrassed a lot and couldn't concentrate on school work. I even had a friend in the seventh grade who I was afraid to see. After about a month or two I was allowed to stay home. No one knew what to do, so I was sent to Child Guidance. For six months, I saw a psychiatrist once a week before the agency closed for summer vacation. I thought I'd go back to her in the Fall when school began again, but I was told I was ineligible since I'd turned 13 and that was the cutoff age. I was left nowhere.

High school brought more of the same panicky feelings. I still felt severe separation anxiety and often felt disoriented and fearful. It didn't help that I was only five feet tall. I had no image of my self and felt small. I was terrified of the world beyond my home, of any thing or any one not familiar to me.

Arrangements were made for my mother to come to school with me. She'd wait for me in the Attendance Coordinators Office. During the day, I'd check to make sure she was there. Sometimes she'd leave early without telling me and I'd have an anxiety attack. I wouldn't tell anybody because I was so embarrassed. I'd also feel enraged at her for deserting me.

My parents took me to different doctors. One told me to suck on a lump of sugar when I felt anxious. One fluoroscoped me, having me drink a liquid as my parents and he stood in front of me to view the show. As the liquid descended, the doctor pointed out various organs and said, "He's very healthy. Nothing wrong with him." When the show was over, he spoke to my parents privately.

I overheard this doctor suggest shock treatments from someone in Manhattan. I ran out of the office when I heard this. Fortunately, my parents didn't think that was a good idea ... or they couldn't afford the electric bill. They continued to seek help from other doctors.

After several months, my mother didn't come to school with me. I had good and bad days, but the anxiety was always there. For a short time I saw a social worker in Manhattan through Catholic Charities. She was a pleasant band-aid but not much more.

In my senior year, I got very anxious again. This time I sought help from a local psychiatrist. There were two on Staten Island at the time. One plugged patients into the electrical outlet and the other gave Calcium Gluconate injections along with minor therapy. Guess which one I chose.

The old German psychiatrist worked out of his home, although his main office was on Park Avenue in Manhattan. His dining room doubled as his waiting room. I'd often find three or four people ahead of me. It was early Group Therapy, although the group diminished by one every twenty minutes or so. He told

"Caffe Della Pace" by A.B. (oil painting)

his patients he didn't like them talking about their problems to each other. Instead, he acted more like a friend with whom you exchanged stories.

He told me of his experiences during World War I when he was a medic for the German Army. In a rare mood, he once sang some of his marching songs. After a brief exchange of conversation (that often depended upon the number of people stacked up behind me in the waiting room) he'd give me my weekly injection. I felt as if a fire surged through my body, head to toes in seconds. Beyond that, I felt nothing. In theory, the injection was supposed to deaden my nervous system. I don't think so.

This doctor once told me that I was one of the worst cases he'd ever seen because I never got a break from anxiety. I never got worse or better with him. Being aware and rational seemed to be negatives in his eyes. But he did relate to me as few men in my life had.

I graduated from high school and received my diploma for the task, even if I'd only attended about two and a half years worth. I grew eight inches in those four years.

During the summers I built houses with my father. We constructed the forms and poured concrete, stripped the forms, and laid the deck. We framed and shingled the house and sometimes we painted the interior. I liked the work, but I probably wouldn't have done it if I had to work for someone I didn't know. I sure couldn't see working for myself. It was too much responsibility with my anxiety. But I was glad I did the work and it was physically beneficial. Building houses was about the only time I related to my father. Maybe it's more accurate to say my father didn't relate to me or anyone else. Maybe he couldn't relate. He was *The Boss*, often distant and cold.

Among my many fears, traveling was a big one. It was difficult for me to leave the Island, and because one can't leave without taking a bridge or ferry, I especially felt the separation. The further away I was from my home, the more fearful and anxious I'd become, especially in places I'd never been before. Change was always a problem. I'd become disoriented.

Not knowing what to do the rest of my life, and not wanting to face the reality of work, I enrolled in a Community

College. I was able to drive anywhere on the Island and it became my playground as well as my prison.

I enjoyed the freedom that college brought with it, different than the restrictions of high school. I asked someone at registration where Home Room was and was very happy to find out I had complete freedom between classes. I knew so little about the world.

After two years at the Community College, I transferred to another local, but private, college on the Island. I had a difficult time adjusting to the change and a lot of my anxiety returned. I dropped down to one or two courses before returning to full time attendance. Because it was hard for me to enter the class, I'd often sit by the door. A sociology professor was understanding of my anxiety. I enjoyed the remaining years in college and made friends with a group of students.

In my first year of college, I'd started seeing a girl I knew in high school. Although I had crushes on one or two girls then, I'd been too shy to speak to them. By this time I'd been seeing the same girl for four years and we had sex often. I was always afraid of getting her pregnant, afraid of the commitment that would mean marriage since pregnancy meant marriage at that time. So I took precautions.

This girl obviously had to have problems to continue seeing me. She was the kind of person who'd conform to whomever she was with, so I never knew her. It was a stormy relationship that ended when she appeared at a friend's house with her husband! Years later I saw a photo of her in the Daily News. Her husband had held her at knife-point for three days until the police rescued her. She had a seven year old daughter. I haven't heard about her since then.

I saw several other girls in college, getting involved with the unhealthy ones because I didn't feel obligated to them. I felt I couldn't handle a woman who wanted normal things, like a functioning, working husband. I liked being with healthier people, but I didn't want anything beyond friendship with them.

I felt more comfortable with people who had problems than those I thought didn't have any. And I preferred those who weren't very conventional. I thought that those kind of people would somehow be able to understand me more. It was less embarrassing telling such people about my fears. I also felt more comfortable with women than with most men.

It took me six years to drift through college. I majored in Sociology and minored in Art. I enjoyed drawing and painting as well as acting. When I look at people I notice all the nuances of their facial expressions. I can hear myself talk to them and be aware of their reaction to me as well as my reaction to them. Once I broke out in laughter because of the way a woman spoke and looked. My friends were embarrassed, but her totality was very funny. It often seems as if I'm on two planes at the same time. This confused me often, especially when I was younger. I received my B.A. in Sociology in 1965.

After I graduated, the Army put me through two physicals. I'd changed therapists several times by then and was armed with a letter. I actually was willing to go in, but I received a deferment.

I felt pretty good during this time and got a job with the city, working as a Street Club Worker. It was a social work job, hanging around street corners with problem kids. My job was to become friends with them and try to divert their activities to socially acceptable ones. I worked with groups of boys and sometimes was able to get them summer jobs through the city. Sometimes they'd come to me at night and tell me their personal problems. I felt I should be more qualified than I was. The agency was formed because of the Gang Wars in the 50's and 60's. When they subsided (and the city had no concept of the future) the agency changed its entire concept and ended the street club workers.

I left the agency before that happened. I could have easily worked for the city like many others who work for 25 years, retire immediately and collect their pension. But at 27, I was in conflict and feeling anxious again, perhaps fearing the commitment of staying at a job I wasn't quite sure of. The sensitivity of my nature may have upset me more than I was aware of.

I worked a bit in construction again and wandered aimlessly. I started seeing a psychiatrist again and went back on Sodium Amytal and therapy. The doctor delved into my morbid

"Madison Avenue Rain" by A.B. (oil painting)

past. Then he decided that I couldn't undergo analysis since I wasn't living or loving ... no job, no girl, no deal.

Without work or a therapist, I returned to a local city college and studied photography and painting. Beautiful shapes and forms always attracted me, whether they be women, automobiles, or homes. I've been equally attracted to calmness and beauty, like that of old homes and tree-lined streets. Everything has a negative or positive aesthetic charge in my eyes. I don't know if this is part of my anxiety or part of my nature. I'm very conscious of everything around me, of being in touch and being off balance. Anxious people seem to feel the difference more. Either way, everything in my life has seemed exaggerated. If the exaggeration is due to my anxiety, then it has had a positive effect on my ability to appreciate many things around me. I've received a second undergraduate degree and become a serious painter.

Over the years, I was given many medications, starting with Miltowns. Next was Stelazine (I don't know why, but it was new and why not try it?) Librium made me uninhibited and tired. Tofranil was effective but the dosage I needed to block anxiety would have killed me because it sped up my heart rate so much. I think a lot of people can be helped by medications and I'm glad they're out there. I know there's a pill somewhere for me, but I've stopped looking for it.

Childhood and adolescence was an extremely difficult time for myself, my parents, and my friends. And reactions to my anxiety by doctors was often primitive. (One of the few suggestions they didn't make was to bore a hole through my skull.) But the outlook for people with anxiety is dramatically better now that it's ever been. Near my home is a group called Freedom From Fear, started by a woman who had anxiety attacks. That clinic (as well as many others around the country and world) has many mental health professionals who are familiar with depression and anxiety disorders. It's good to know understanding now exists if you need it.

I've somehow managed to do what I want to do, in spite of myself. I have no regrets, despite anxiety's interference. For decades I felt so much anxiety and panic about what was going to happen if I did this or that or went here or there, but *nothing awful ever did happen.* There still is anxiety and sometimes panic to deal with, but it has become less important in the whole scheme of things; as years pass, I'm able to do more with less anxiety.

I'm in my early fifties now and I spend most of my time painting. As I've explored new forms of self expression, I've learned to understand why I view things as I do. Having a direction and purpose has allowed my anxiety to subside and has made me a stronger individual. Because of my art, I have found myself and, for the first time, have been able to take control of my life.

Escape From the
Prison Without Walls
by Denise Ranauro

When I started driving at seventeen, I was fearless and daring. Without any hesitation, I drove anywhere, anytime, and in any weather. My friends would jump into my beautiful blue convertible and we would cruise around just for fun. Like most teens, I reveled in this new freedom. I could shop 'til I dropped or go wherever I desired.

On a beautiful day in May 1978, my life changed drastically in an instant. I was twenty-five, the mother of a two-year-old son and six months pregnant with my second child. I was driving home on the highway from my part time job. Minutes before, I began to feel tense. Thinking I was just anxious about getting home to be with my son, I ignored this uneasiness. The anxiety started to intensify. Tremors, light-headedness, sweating and intense pounding of my heart overtook me. My limbs seemed to be paralyzed and I was certain that I would lose control of my car. Fright progressed to terror. Death seemed imminent. In a moment I'd entered the prison without walls; to be incarcerated for well over a decade.

Frantic and confused, I somehow managed to ease the car onto the shoulder of the road. As I turned up the air conditioner to the highest level, my head dropped to rest on the steering wheel. Taking deep breaths of the cold air, I attempted to revive myself, to "snap out of it." It seemed as if I was there a long time, but in reality, it was probably about fifteen minutes. Not one person stopped to offer assistance.

Mustering every bit of strength I had left, I barely regained enough composure to maneuver to the nearby exit. Ever so carefully, I drove home through the local streets, the aftermath still plaguing me. It was as if I had entered another dimension;

something I had never experienced before, a sense of unreality held me captive. The degree of force carved itself in my memory.

On the next visit to my obstetrician I related the episode to him. He told me that this was nature's way of telling me, through my body, to stop driving for the remainder of the pregnancy. If I had heeded this advice, I would have never driven again. Intuition told me the what he was saying wasn't true. I felt patronized and I continued to drive locally, despite my fear of a recurrence. Sometimes I'd feel extremely anxious while other times I felt only mild tension. Who would take over my responsibilities? Self-sufficiency was necessary for me and the ability to drive was part of this.

In the mid-seventies, panic disorder was not yet a diagnosis. My family physician attributed these symptoms to the stress of being the mother of two young children along with my desire to do my best rearing them. The parade of pills commenced. I was given low doses of an anti-anxiety drug that helped only occasionally. My infant had colic and neither slept through the night (until the age of three) nor did he nap. As my condition worsened with the onset of insomnia, tremors, and stomach spasms, I now needed to take more medication. Sleeping and anti-spasmodic drugs were added to my prescription list. Taking three different pills at once offered no relief. When these remedies failed, I was given an antidepressant drug. It was noted on my medical record that I was depressed, but that I had good insight. All things considered, was it any wonder why I was depressed?

In the ensuing years, I had remissions and relapses. At times, I did not make a connection between the events in my life and recurrence of attacks. This revelation would come later and prove to be a blessing in my battle.

It wasn't until the mid-eighties that my doctor told me I was having panic attacks. By this time, the disorder was presenting itself frequently and began to occur in situations other than driving my car. I was panicking on escalators, crossing main roads, in high places, and generally anyplace where there was no immediate escape. It was especially disturbing when I tried to walk down the floating dock at the marina to see my brother's new boat and I wasn't able to, even with someone holding my arm. On the road to agoraphobia, I declared war against this incapacitating incarceration. Although I wasn't sure I would win, I wasn't going to give up without a fight.

The medication was changed and the dosage increased. My ability to function was minimal. Gradually I improved but the fear of these attacks caused anticipatory anxiety and hampered any further progress. More often than not, I avoided any situation in which I expected to panic. I'd always been a freedom-loving, independent person. To me this debilitation was humiliating and extremely frustrating.

If I had an attack at a certain intersection, I'd drive a different route the next time. I became very adept at eluding possible sites of occurrences. Traffic lights and driving in the center and left lanes were particularly unnerving. I avoided these, too. Sometimes I'd have to pull over and let other cars pass because of my fear of being in the middle of moderate to heavy traffic.

From childhood to adulthood, I have had more than my share of problems to deal with. The childhood conflicts, I believe, did not cause the panic. Because I am a very spiritual person, I had faith that I would be rewarded with peace in my adult life, but my adult life did not turn out as I anticipated. There were many serious, though sporadic problems that concerned my marriage. One year I felt secure, and the next, I didn't. I noticed a correlation between these times and the remissions and recurrences of my panic attacks. I realized this much later on and it would help in my fight against the phobia. I may be biologically predisposed to panic, but psychological conflict, I came to believe, played a major role in the disorder.

After fourteen years on the roller coaster ride of marriage, I sought the help of a therapist. I was blessed to find one who would play a major role in my fight to ward off the attacks. The purpose of the first visit was to discuss my marital problems. In conversation, I mentioned my disorder. He, too, felt that it was related to the conflicts.

Dealing with a professional gave me some peace of mind. This was serious business and I felt that I was now doing every-thing possible to help myself. The abilities of my therapist to calm me were incredible. During this time, I was able to almost wean off medication entirely. The dosage was down to one milligram a day. I was willing to try anything. Hypnosis rendered me so calm that after the session, I almost drove onto the entrance to the highway.

I could not afford the cost of therapy forever. After various relaxation techniques were taught, and all the insight I could possibly gain was now mine, the regular visits became occasional. The reason for the attacks was that I was trapped in circumstances that were beyond my control. Once I understood this I knew that I was sane and was capable of dealing with the disorder on my own.

Despite my expectation, the number of attacks as well as the dosage of my medication, crept up very slowly. Nevertheless, I was able to lessen the severity with the skills I acquired in therapy. It was necessary to chauffeur my sons, and sometimes their friends, to baseball games and other activities. Even when I began to feel an attack coming on, I'd use these tactics to either stop or lessen the panic. No one riding in the car had a clue of what I was going through. I was trying not to impress my children, fearing that they would develop the phobia eventually.

I thought of ways that would enable me to change my circumstances and solve my problems. With the encouragement of my therapist, I entered college at the age of thirty-five. I have always enjoyed learning. To my surprise, I adjusted quickly to the campus environment and attained excellent grades. I attended a local university for two and a half years as a part time student while working part time and caring for my family.

In the last semester I attended, the problems at home accelerated. Panic overcame me worse than ever in my life. Fighting the symptoms drained me more than the attacks. I stopped driving in July of 1990. To get to my job and attend school, I had to take four buses each way. In the sweltering heat, waiting as long as forty-five minutes for one bus put even more stress on me. Eventually, I dropped out of school. It felt as if I had hit rock-bottom and I was fairly sure that I would never recover.

A few weeks later, there was an advertisement in the local newspaper. It was placed by a research clinic based near my home. They were seeking volunteers to participate in a study of an experimental drug for those who suffer from panic disorder. At that point I was willing to try anything. I immediately called and went through the interview process. Because this was a double blind study, the subject had to be willing to take an unknown drug. Neither the research physician, nor the patient would know which drug was being taken until the end of the study. There were three possible treatments: a placebo, a medication that has been on the market for some time, or the experimental drug. I knew in a short time that I was not being given the placebo. My body is extremely sensitive and the panic went into remission. The eight weeks or so passed and the study ended. I learned that I had been taking the experimental drug. Ironically, this turned out to be the only drug that provided relief and produced no side effects in me. Four years later, it has yet to receive FDA approval. The compensation for participation in the study was free treatment for six months to stabilize the patient on a medication that is currently used in treatment.

More problems surfaced. One by one, every possible drug was prescribed for me, and each had worse side effects than the one before. These were quite serious. My blood pressure dropped drastically; at one point it was 70/56. I fell down often, constantly dizzy and weak. Next came weight loss. I was 110 pounds with no extra weight to spare. Another side effect interfered with my writing ability. I constantly skipped letters as I wrote words. The list of drugs administered and the side effects seemed endless. I wondered what all of this was doing to my body. After determining that I could not tolerate any of these medications, I was placed back on the anti-anxiety medication and my treatment at the clinic was ended.

My participation in the study wasn't a waste of time; the relief obtained from the trial drug gave me the confidence to attempt to drive again. Each morning at five or six o'clock, when the roads were clear of traffic, I'd get in my car and drive. I initially drove one block and went home. I then drove around the block each day for one week before venturing onto the main road. It was done gradually but with the persistence of a high-pressure salesman. I refused to give up. Strange as it may seem, I had a vendetta against the disorder for disrupting my life.

This alone was tough to do. But I had another strike against me. I was experiencing a period of the worst luck I have ever had in my life. I leased a new car, thinking that I would enjoy driving it and this would avert the anxiety. The day after I got the car, I was rear-ended, extremely hard, just six blocks from my home, by a careless driver. When I saw no damage to the car, I felt safe.

Less than three weeks later I ventured to the supermarket. Everything was fine until I exited the parking lot. A pickup came along; it seemed to appear from out of nowhere and hit my car broadside. This happened on a very busy street. I'd just started to gain confidence again and someone's carelessness diminished it in seconds, leaving me panicked, shaken up, and confused. For the first time in my life, I stuttered. Someone else had to call the police. In my irrational state, I blamed the car for being jinxed.

On to another psychiatrist. My choices of providers were limited by my health plan. The first doctor prescribed a few medications that were new on the market. Again, the side effects were too severe to bear. After about three new drugs were tried, we agreed that I should go back to taking only the anti-anxiety drug. In addition, I was so worn out that he suggested I take a liquid vitamin. I later found out that it contained alcohol. What a dangerous combination. I couldn't figure out why I felt sleepier than normal and this explained it. I would imagine that it was equally frustrating for the doctor to be unsuccessful in his attempt to help me. After a while, the physician had taken on so many patients, (he also worked full time at a health care facility) that our attempts to make appointments became nearly impossible. In fact, I was supposed to see him every two weeks and he had no openings for the next four weeks. No effort was made to fit me in. I ended my treatment with this doctor feeling totally disheartened. I wondered if any health professional, besides my therapist, cared about the patient, not just the fee. I kept returning to my therapist every time I needed a boost of support and he always made every effort to fit me into his extremely busy schedule.

I had a list of four choices to provide me with treatment. The next doctor was contacted. After reciting my lengthy history in perfect detail from memory, I was informed of a fact that I had never known; the physician told me that I was one of a small percentage of patients who could not tolerate any of these drugs. I wish I had been told that before. It would have saved me from many unpleasant effects. We agreed that I should stay on my current prescription, and if necessary, the dosage could be raised. The only effect I had to endure was sleepiness, which was tolerable.

While in college, I had taken two psychology courses. One was introductory and the other was about experimental topics. My term paper for the latter course was done on Panic Disorder. I did an enormous amount of research compared to the scope of the paper. I was eager to learn all that I possibly could about my disorder. Pouring through professional journals, books, magazines, and any other media I could find, I discovered a wealth of information on the subject. One study correlated the onset of panic with psychological conflicts in life events. I thought I was reading my life story. In so many ways, this helped me because it gave me all the viewpoints and findings, both psychological and biological, that I would use as tools in my attempt to fight the disorder. Naturally, my grade on the paper was an "A." Who is better qualified to write a term paper on the phobia than one who suffers from it?

I dropped out of college, left a high-paying job as controller of a construction related company, and did a minimal amount of chores at home. I'd lost all my strength and felt I would never be the same energetic, bubbly person I'd once been. I did a little freelance work at home, but I didn't want to work anymore and I loathed the cooking, laundry, and house cleaning I had to do. Activities I once enjoyed no longer interested me.

Miracles do happen, though. My strength began to return when I kept reminding myself that I had two sons to raise. Even though teenagers, there was still important work to do in raising them. I knew that my constant state of depression made them sad. They alternated between efforts to cheer me up and wanting to be away from me.

This is when I seriously began questioning each and every aspect of my life. I became even more perceptive to the effects sustained by those around me. The whole picture was clear. If I could have given in without affecting anyone, I probably would have. But this was not possible. Instead of burying them, I faced my conflicts head on, no matter what the consequences were to me. I accepted the reality of my inability to change certain things. I did all I could to regain faith in myself and my religion, and I hoped for the best outcome.

As a result, a sense of serenity began to emerge. Still feeling the constant tension and anxiety, I decided to at least try my best. On most days, once I started driving, the tension abated. This amazed me. I know that I will probably always habitually anticipate.

When the signs of an attack began, I'd divert my attention from whatever I felt was causing it. After these tactics brought success, it reinforced my confidence and determination. I no longer avoided everything altogether; I dared to conquer certain fears by thinking rationally. I had to run the gamut before I could get near my goal of overcoming this disabling phobia. I still cannot drive on highways or bridges, but I can drive to the places I need to.

I derive so much pleasure from watching my teenage sons drive as calmly and carefree as I once did. My prayer is that they will never be afflicted with panic or any other disorder. Even though they may have inherited the predisposition from me, I hope that their lives are always free of the emotional turmoil that I've endured.

Only those who suffer from phobias such as panic and other related disorders truly know the havoc it can wreak in their lives and the effects it can have on their families. This dreaded affliction can cause depression, hopelessness, and ultimately, resignation. I've related my story to illustrate that there is hope if people are unwavering in their determination to help themselves.

I know I'm not permanently released from this prison yet. But I've worked my way to the outside and am breathing the fresh air. Someday I may be able to drive the highway to lead me away from the prison permanently. The view is so much nicer from here and the sight of the full horizon awaits in the days to come.

Postscript:

Although there are still many stressful things going on in my life, I've managed to cut my medication down. This afternoon, I was driving in an area that I do not go to often as I have no need to. Absentmindedly, I turned onto a road that is the entrance to a highway. Suddenly, I found myself driving the expressway for the first time in more than seventeen years. The part that is strange is that this is the same stretch of road where my first panic attack occurred in 1978.

There was no way to turn around and get off. The next exit is three miles away. I thought I would panic for sure. I didn't. Instead, I merely felt tense. I was able to drive about two miles and then pulled onto the shoulder of the road. Not because I was having an attack, but to prevent one. Within minutes, I felt calm enough to drive to the next exit, the same one I drove off back then. Ironically, the name of the exit is Victory Boulevard. I'm still stunned by this incident and wanted to share it. In each victory, no matter how trivial it may seem to others, there is even more hope and confidence instilled in those of us with phobias. I believe we are given signs in mysterious ways. To me, this was a sign that I will once again enjoy the complete freedom of my pre-phobic days. My fondest wish is that everyone has such an uplifting experience.

Fred has an unfortunate experience on the way to getting his Xanax prescription filled.

Getting to the Other Side
by Carolyn Johnson

LEFT TURNS AT RED LIGHTS...

The familiar tension above my shoulder blade was making its presence known as I drove. I kept massaging the area the best I could. That had always helped a little, but this tension was occurring more and more often. I'd often thought it might be bursitis; something was definitely going on there.

The tension spread up behind my neck. I wasn't feeling particularly upbeat as I drove, either. Before leaving the house, I'd had a falling out with a good friend over the telephone. I later wondered if that stress played a part in predisposing me to what was about to take place.

The traffic light ahead was turning to red. I was in the left lane where I could go straight or turn left. As I braked, the tension in my shoulder and neck swiftly spread to other areas. My arms became rigid as boards. My legs stiffened. My neck, head, and eyes seemed paralyzed and locked. This complete body lock had never happened to me before. The red light became interminable. I tapped the brake pedal, letting my car edge forward little by little, in hopes it would somehow speed up the light's changing. I felt as though people in the other cars were all staring at me, mocking the fool. In reality, probably no one noticed me. Then the hyperventilation hit. I tried to steady my breath, yet it was so shallow that I felt I couldn't. I remember thinking that drowning must feel like this. The monster had a grip on me and the light was never going to change.

When the green arrow finally flashed, I got my toes to react. That was the one area in my body I could persuade to perform. I'm sure I must have sped through that left light. I maneuvered the streets as fast as I possibly could until I reached the turnpike entrance. All this transpired in three or four minutes, but it seemed like an hour to me. Once on the turnpike, I raced on. I couldn't even blink my eyes; I was afraid that if I tried, they'd remain shut. I stared straight ahead, my body unable to move, my gasps for breath still continuing. It was five minutes to my exit.

I finally drove down the exit ramp and crossed over to a street free of traffic; the street that led to my home. The second that I arrived on this street, every symptom I'd endured for the past fifteen minutes completely disappeared. My breathing became normal and my body relaxed. My eyes could blink again. I drove the rest of the way home, pulled in the driveway, and wearily got out of the car, totally exhausted. Inside the house, I sat down and allowed myself to cry it out, releasing fear and frustration. Then I got out paper and pen and proceeded to write down all I could remember of what had happened to me.

That was the day I knew what "it" was. I could now put a name to all of the symptoms I had been experiencing. They'd built up into this explosion. I now knew what a full-blown panic attack felt like.

WHY?

Ten years before experiencing that explosive panic attack, my mother-in-law and my sister-in-law died. I was 45 years old and had never lost anyone close to me before. My sister-in-law, Bev, had been my best friend. She was the one person I was free to tell everything to, including all my dreams and fears. With Bev gone, so was my expression of thoughts and feelings.

The next year, my beloved parents died within five days of each other. My mother had been sick for five months before her death; my father died unexpectedly of a heart attack on his way to visit her in the hospital.

I sat at my father's funeral service, staring at the pattern of the carpet. The design seemingly jumped up and hit me in the eyeballs, a very strange first symptom. (A few weeks later, the same thing happened while bowling. Except that time it was the alley I was in that seemingly hit me.)

I think I began shutting out a lot of new relationships by telling myself that no one could measure up to the people I had lost. On the outside I appeared normal, but inside, where no one could see, I was different. I was sad and not letting anyone see it. I wanted to appear stalwart and plucky. My husband was probably the only one who noticed how I'd changed. He'd seen my sadness at the deaths, but I didn't even confide in him as to how badly I felt.

Not expressing my grief prepared to take its toll on my body and mind. All the symptoms I'd experienced for nine years amassed and gathered together, culminating into that massive panic attack at a red light on a nice spring day.

JELLY LEGS

I was raised by parents who never let it be known if they ever suffered pain or hurt. They endured pain without complaining and so did I. I didn't share my symptoms with anyone. During the first few years, my symptoms occurred at intervals. The in-between time was normal and usually made me forget the weird times ... or made me believe they were gone forever.

When I started experiencing "jelly legs" in stores, malls, and any line I had to wait in, I thought my legs had contracted some horrible disease. I had no idea why my legs went weak inside a building, yet were fine when I stepped outside.

About ten months after my parents' deaths, I entered a department store with my shopping list. It was Christmas-time. I selected a couple of good choices and suddenly felt as though a gripping fear had enveloped me. My legs felt weak. I was terrified. I quickly learned the "fight or flight" response; I had to get OUT of that store. I left my shopping cart in mid-aisle and hurriedly left. (Hurriedly is an understatement.) I FLEW out of that store and would become adept in the future at flying out of places whenever necessary. With my seemingly inherited custom of not showing the public-at-large my true discomfort, all the store customers noticed was that I was a lady in a hurry, nothing more. My husband got used to my exciting moments in stores when we shopped together. "My legs are going," I'd tell him. That was his signal that I was about to fly out.

VODKA BECOMES MY CHUM

After a few years of my "strange sensations," I stayed on alert for these feelings to appear. I had to be wary. They could appear out of the blue almost anywhere. Then I discovered how a couple of shots of vodka worked wonders. Before going bowling, for instance, I'd not only bowl superbly, but I'd not even think of the weird sensations appearing. I wasn't about to go to a doctor at that point, fearing a brain tumor would be found or that my legs were withering away. Vodka helped me forget I had such fears. With vodka, my legs held up quite well. And when I golfed, I discovered that a small flask in my golf cart was just the "caddy" I needed to help me through off moments on the fairways. My spells were something no one in the world would understand if I were ever to enlist anyone's confidence. I thought all the strangeness I underwent was unique only to me. Alcohol is so consuming; after using it so often for my outdoor activities, I began using it at home whenever I had an anxious thought.

One late afternoon I began to prepare dinner before my husband was due home. I'd taken two shots of vodka to relax and then put a pot of water on the range to boil. The vodka hit me very strongly and I went upstairs to the bedroom to lie down. I forgot about the boiling pot and quickly fell asleep. I awoke a half hour later and saw what appeared to be a heavy fog. I remembered the pot and realized smoke was filling the house. I rescued the pot and opened all the doors and windows, choking and coughing. Luckily, no fire started and I wasn't harmed. By the time my husband got home, all the evidence was gone. However, the experience of what might have been affected me deeply; I stopped using alcohol to solve my problems that day. It had taken a potentially fatal event for me to realize what I'd been doing.

RESTAURANTS BECOME FORBIDDEN TERRITORY

It was a sunny day. I sang as I drove to a birthday luncheon at a restaurant where I was going to meet three friends. I felt relaxed and at peace with the world and I hadn't drunk any alcohol.

As my friends chatted, I became conscious of the tension in back of my neck. I began rubbing it, but the spasms got worse.

I'd never had any problems in restaurants before. But my shoulders tensed and I had trouble maneuvering my neck from side to side. My friends laughed and talked, but I became more visibly uncomfortable. I looked at one of my friends and told her I didn't feel well and had to go outside. She accompanied me and I felt better as soon as I stepped out. After a few minutes, I went back into the restaurant, believing I'd be fine. But I was wrong. Everything flared back and worsened. My legs started shaking. My friends asked what was wrong, so I became embarrassed on top of everything else. Never had I displayed an attack in front of others. They asked questions, but I had no answers. I pleaded with them to go on with their meals that had just arrived. They sensed I was embarrassed and turned their attention to each other. After about ten minutes my attack lessened and I felt better. I joined in the fun and we all forgot about my shenanigans, but I couldn't forget that people had witnessed my attack this time. That made a difference to me.

The next day I asked my husband to make an appointment for me with his doctor. I wanted a complete physical. I asked my husband to do it because I thought I'd chicken out doing it. He was happy I finally was going to do something about myself. But I felt terrified ... afraid of finding out what really was wrong with me. It'd be a long time before even thinking about going into another restaurant.

A-OK, BUT NOW I CAN'T DRIVE

I presented the doctor with a description of all the symptoms I'd had. He read it and said he couldn't say what I had until he examined me and gave me various tests. It turned out that I passed all the tests I was given. The doctor said that I should get rid of the stress I was under. I certainly would've liked to do that except my stress was from the physical symptoms. I was glad to pass the physical, but I still had no answers for my attacks.

It was a few days after my visit to the doctor that I had the attack at the red light. I'd heard and read about panic attacks before. Maybe it was the process of elimination after the physical, but I knew after being at the red light that that was what I'd had. It now had a name.

The panic attacks were not finished with me yet. There was one more "lulu" waiting for me. After the incident at the red light, I became unable to drive my car at all. If I tried, spasms and cramps would begin in the back of my neck and spread to my limbs. I'd freeze with fear. I attempted to drive but couldn't make it out of my driveway.

Inside my house I began getting attacks if I sat at the dining table. I thought this was connected to the restaurant episode. Attacks began occurring in other situations; speaking on the telephone and riding as a passenger in a car. I felt desperate and depressed. I managed to get to the golf course a few times by breathing into a paper bag along the way. It was important to me to continue this one activity.

I used the paper bag for only a couple of weeks because I was about to be saved.

THE AD IN THE PAPER

I'd seen the advertisement in the local paper about a Support Group for agoraphobics and people who experienced panic attacks. My husband drove me to the school where the meeting was held and helped me find the room. I was pretty nervous, entering the room with my usual "jelly legs." There were four other people there and we exchanged symptoms. Some of them discussed medications which I knew nothing about. Carrie handed me a book to read; *Simple Effective Treatment for Agoraphobia* by Claire Weekes.

I began reading the book when I got home and I didn't stop until 2 a.m. Saying that the revelations were astounding is putting it mildly. I made notes of all the parts that rang a bell with me and there were many. My most important discovery was that I was causing the worst parts of my attacks and that there were ways I could stop this. There were tools I could use to drive again. The whole secret was to learn to accept the panic when it came and to train myself to relax and let it come ... just let it happen. If I could learn this, I could be free of the panic.

I read until my eyes closed from tiredness and began reading more in the morning. There was a section in the book about driving and how to overcome the fear of it. Dr. Weekes wrote about accepting my panic and not looking at the miles to be covered on any trip, but just coping with and staying in the moment.

Something astonishing happened. I could get out of my driveway and onto the street. Guided by a tape and my newfound knowledge. I could drive my car again. Although still afraid of getting out into traffic again, I did well on the back roads. I was grateful I'd gone to the meeting the night before.

I started applying my new knowledge to the attacks I felt in the house. I began feeling at ease sitting at the table and talking on the phone. I entered stores and let my body relax, feeling half of the former uncomfortable sensations.

The book told me to practice, and practice I did. I read many other books on the subject from the library. I made copious notes and made more tapes to play in the car. By the time I went to the next group meeting, I'd made dramatic changes. I drove by myself again and had very little jelly legs symptom. I learned how to breathe slowly and deeply to avoid hyperventilating.

Carrie told me she'd gone to the Mental Health Clinic for her panic attacks and had been put on an antidepressant drug along with talk therapy. She said this treatment had helped her recover. I decided I'd do the same.

By this time, there were only two things I couldn't bring myself to do; drive the expressway and eat in restaurants. I resisted these situations. I did attempt driving the turnpike once, but I got so nervous and jumpy that I had to get off it. Restaurants were still out of the question. I began seeing a psychiatrist which was something I'd never dreamed I'd do.

TREATMENT BEGINS

Dr. Benton was a warm, friendly bear of a man, complete with a woolly beard. He asked many questions before diagnosing me with Panic Disorder, then prescribed an antidepressant, Norpramin. He thought I'd done a lot of work on myself and seemed genuinely sorry that I couldn't go in restaurants or drive the expressway. And he told me the medication would allow me to do these things, but I shouldn't expect results for three weeks or so. There'd be subtle changes, he said, and I'd feel like doing things I hadn't felt like doing for a long time.

During the first week of taking the medication, I felt about the same as I had ... anxious. Nothing changed. On the seventh day, however, I wanted to go up on the turnpike and see what it would be like to drive on it. Just the day before, wild horses wouldn't have gotten me there.

I entered the highway and felt absolutely no anxiety. I drove about three miles and took an exit. Then I re-entered for the return ride. It felt wonderful driving along so freely; I began yelling to myself how great it was. A motorcyclist passed me and I waved to him. I grinned as I was euphoric. Driving was as it had been before I'd even heard of panic attacks. I wasn't supposed to feel any changes for three weeks, yet just after a week I felt a miracle had occurred.

I began driving to different places, listening to my driving tape continuously. I was dependent on that tape for the next three months; it was my crutch that made driving in comfort possible. And then I didn't need to hear it anymore. What a joy to listen to my music cassettes again. I'd missed them a lot.

I had therapy sessions with a caring psychologist. She helped me deal with a lot of anger and resentment I hadn't even realized I'd been harboring. They'd contributed to the panic attacks. Most importantly, my psychologist helped me deal with the grief over those deaths I'd experienced.

RESTAURANTS CONQUERED

After the delight of driving again, I decided to work on conquering my other bugaboo, the dreaded restaurants. My husband and I usually shopped on Saturdays and we agreed that I'd try to go to a restaurant on that day each week. The first experience this time around wasn't too bad. I'd explained to him how I rated my anxiety on a scale of one to ten in different situations. This helped me a lot when he'd ask me what "number" I was at in the restaurants.

By the third or fourth time, my ratings were a nice and steady "zero." When I did feel tension, I'd use the deep breathing exercises to make the tension release and my body relax.

BECOMING THE FACILITATOR

I looked forward to the Support Group meetings. It gave me a sense of security to know Carrie would be waiting there to guide the rest of us.

One day I received a letter from her, catching me by surprise. She wrote that she had to relinquish her role as Facilitator. She was regretful, but there were problems that she had to take care of. I was astonished when she suggested I take over as Facilitator. She said she had full confidence in me and that seemed to build my confidence in myself. I wrote back that I'd miss her terribly, but I'd do my best to keep the meetings going. I felt I'd been nurtured and now was taking the role of the nurturer.

I was quite nervous the night of the next meeting. I got there early in order to calm myself and practice deep breathing. Three people showed up and I discovered that conversation isn't difficult to keep going when in a group of agoraphobics. I'd worried about that before and learned I worried needlessly. The things we all had in common was the catalyst for keeping the talk moving. It always is. The need for all of us to verbalize and externalize our fears and concerns is ever present; we must talk it out and be willing to listen to each other. The coping techniques we've learned individually must be shared with others. Any knowledge we have should be passed on as we're the only people who can truly understand and sympathize.

After becoming the Facilitator, I met many people with agoraphobia and panic disorder. They were all ages and had different personalities, but all were bright and most of them worked hard at overcoming their condition. I made many lasting friendships in that group.

FAST FORWARDING TO NOW

Five years have passed since that full-blown panic attack at the red light. Many changes have taken place. In 1991, my husband took a job in Virginia and we moved from our home in New England. When he retired a year ago, we decided to remain in Virginia as we'd come to love our new home. We've driven back and forth many times to visit friends and family. I've driven the 600 mile trip myself, over bridges, through tunnels, and on five-lane expressways. I guess you could say my driving phobia has been conquered.

When I moved to Virginia, I started a support group. I've found people are more reticent about coming forward with their problems here. We live in an area that is more slow-paced than in the North, and perhaps the less stressful atmosphere is more conducive to lower anxiety.

It took awhile to establish the group, but now there are three members who attend regularly. Working together, we've been able to establish empathy and trust and are benefiting each other. The people I've met reinforce my own inner strength and are as much support for me as I am for them. The tapes I made for myself have been copied and distributed (through advertisements in newsletters) helping many people all over the country. I would've never dreamed this five years ago.

I stayed on the antidepressant for four years. With the help of my doctor, I tried to lower the dosage. But while looking at greeting cards in a drugstore, I was suddenly struck by a jolting panic attack. I'd thought this would never happen to me again. I made my way out of the store on my old jelly legs with much dismay and despair. After about two weeks, I went back to see my doctor who put me back on the former dosage.

This relapse set into motion a new education for me in the sage of panic disorder. I recalled a doctor once saying how we are never through with panic attacks, we simply go into "remission" from them. I also recalled my doctor in Connecticut telling me that although I felt reborn and free of all panic, I shouldn't rule out the possibility of any future attacks. I had to teach myself that I could be subject to them. One doesn't *get over* panic attacks as much as learns to get *in control* of them.

After I accepted this new knowledge, I practiced the old techniques for relaxing again. I started achieving the status I had at the time before the relapse. My confidence returned and my anxiety leveled out.

I felt more sure than the previous time that this was the time to go for it. I tapered my medication for several months, eventually to a zero level. It was a pretty smooth transition. The moments of anxiety have been there, but nothing has lasted long. Most episodes occur when I haven't slept well the night before or when I've become too busy and have let stress seep in. I usually can account for the reason.

In 1994, I was asked to try out for playing piano in a local band that plays gospel music. This has worked out well and gives me much enjoyment and fulfillment to have music be an integral part of my life. I've noticed that while performing and even during rehearsals, there've been times when I've felt my adrenaline soar and my muscles tense. But the sensations subside after uncomfortably running their course. I'm convinced that this occurs from my feeling overly joyful by the music. My body then produces too much adrenaline. My education continues.

Despite this occurring, I couldn't nor wouldn't let these sensations deter me from pursuing my musical venture. I believe I'll be subject to these incidents for the rest of my life, but that's okay now. I've no fear of it. I'm at that plateau where having a panic attack is of little consequence to me. I function normally with many activities, and I don't let the possibility of having another one interfere with my plans.

I believe anyone can overcome panic and anxiety with diligence and practice, practice, practice. I've pretty much learned to stay in the moment. That took practice before becoming automatic. I can breathe deeply and make myself relax. Once getting to the other side of panic, you can gain the confidence of knowing you can always survive. Gaining control means the absence of fear.

I've made changes in my personality and I'm a different person than I was five years ago. But I like this person better, over here on the other side.

What are the symptoms of a panic attack?

Typically, a panic attack may feel as if it comes out of nowhere, while a person is doing an ordinary activity like driving or walking. Suddenly, a barrage of frightening and uncomfortable symptoms may occur, including some or all of the following:

racing or pounding heartbeat

chest pains

dizziness or light-headedness

nausea

flushes or chills

difficulty breathing

tingling or numbness in the hands

feelings of unreality

terror

fear of going "crazy" or losing control

fear of dying

Information provided by the National Institute of Mental Health (NIMH) booklet "Understanding Panic Disorder"

Sleeping With One Eye Open
by Molly Matteson

I was just a little girl, eight years of age, when I experienced my first flash of panic. Before I could get to the safety of my mother's arms, it vanished as quickly as it had come. Even in that young mind, I somehow knew it was the beginning of something very frightening.

Through junior and senior high school, I continued to experience brief bouts of panic. Although they were very scary, they didn't last very long and there were often long periods of time between attacks when I felt just like any normal kid going through puberty.

Fast forward to 1968 .... I met my first husband, a Marine, and accompanied him from Missouri to Tennessee to California with no problem. I will admit, however that my first experience with California freeway gridlock was very anxiety-producing. Shortly after arriving, I interviewed for and was hired as a legal secretary in a large local law firm.

In 1971, Mr. Marine and I divorced. I met a Santa Ana police officer and we were married in 1972. The next five years were a very dark time in my life. My new husband was Dr. Jekyll/Mr. Hyde in disguise—the most generous, caring person at times but when the switch was thrown, he became both physically and mentally abusive. As the incidents of abuse escalated, so did my panic attacks. Of course, I didn't know they were panic attacks, I just knew something was happening to me and it felt exactly the same as that very first time in the side yard of my house when I was eight years old.

That began several years of being referred to different doctors, being prescribed different medications (tranquilizers, muscle relaxants, hormones, anti-seizure drugs, etc.) and undergoing endless tests, from brain scans to EKGs and everything in between. The verdict? I was perfectly healthy and it was "all in my head." Personally, I chalked it up to five years of abuse and unhappiness. After all, when I divorced my husband in 1977, the panic attacks started to dwindle away.

Soon after the divorce, I took a two week trip to Europe, enrolled in an evening college course, and met the third significant man in my life. He was a "keeper" and I was extremely happy and content. Then, in 1986, the panic attacks came back with ferocity and completely "out of the blue." We were planning to drive out to the desert on a Saturday morning to visit my boyfriend's son and daughter-in-law. The minute I woke up, I knew something was wrong but tried to ignore it, thinking those feelings would go away as they always had. But they continued to get worse. Five miles down the freeway, I told him I had to go home NOW! He asked why and could only tell him that I was sick and had to get home immediately. He took me back and as soon as we pulled in the driveway, the physical symptoms started to subside. Once inside the house, I was pretty much okay.

Two weeks later, just before a trip to Las Vegas, I experienced a serious panic attack at work. I called my doctor and told him about the failed trip to the desert and that I was now afraid to drive to Las Vegas for the weekend. He told me he wanted to change my medication from Centrax to Xanax because it would help me more with my nerves. I did manage to make the trip to Las Vegas, but because of a business commitment that required my boyfriend to continue on to Denver, I flew from Vegas back to Orange County. I was in the air exactly 52 minutes and it was the longest 52 minutes of my life. To this day, I remember doing some pretty strange things on that airplane to keep from going "crazy." I ordered coffee and told the flight attendant to take it back. I ordered a glass of orange juice and couldn't get it down. I took everything out of my purse and put it back, took it out again and put it back, over and over and over. I cannot imagine what the person sitting next to me must have thought, but I didn't care; I was totally concentrated on making it back home in one mental piece.

I saw my doctor the next day, prepared to tell him this was much more than a case of nerves. He was affiliated with a teaching hospital and asked if I would mind if a medical student sat in on the examination. As soon as I described the two trips, the student looked at me and said, "You have agoraphobia." HOO-RAY! Now I had a name for what I was experiencing. But what did it mean? At that time, unfortunately, it meant continuing on Xanax with no thought to any kind of therapy. I started reading everything I could get my hands on about agoraphobia and panic disorder and began trying some of the relaxation techniques contained in those books.

Between that and the Xanax, I got to a point that I called "manageable." In other words, I was able to make it back and forth to work and perform my duties. I also could go out to a movie or to dinner with my boyfriend, but never, ever was I comfortable with those activities. Always lurking in the back of my mind was—what if "it" happens again?

Changes were made at the law firm, where I had now been working 18 years; a smaller law firm merged into ours and there were switches in management and in job descriptions. It was a mess from the start and rapidly deteriorated into a "them versus us" attitude. I had worked my way up to corporate paralegal over the years and now found myself in the position of also being assigned as secretary to three other attorneys in different fields for law. The workload and process of learning new duties were overwhelming, but if I said anything, I was reported as having a "bad attitude." If I asked advice from other secretaries about the proper filing of court documents, I was reported as "socializing too much." When I received my annual review, for the first time in 18 years I was marked "unsatisfactory" even though I received glowing reviews in the area of work with which I was familiar.

In the space of one year, I had been called on the carpet so many times that the sound of the office manager's voice was enough to trigger a panic attack. I was harassed by the managing partner, told I was worthless, asked why I didn't just quit, and threatened with termination "if I didn't keep my head down and mouth shut." I also lost my mother to pancreatic cancer and my father to congestive heart failure the same year.

Everything came to a head a few days before my two-week Christmas vacation. The attorneys that I had worked with for so long decided to break off and join another law firm. I was ecstatic. Unfortunately, on the day before my vacation, I was told that my immediate supervisor had chosen to stay and I had no choice but to stay, also.

I made an appointment with my doctor (a new one) who increased my dosage of Xanax and recommended I see the HMO's psychologist. I started treatment with the psychologist that week. He was a nice guy, but somewhat limited in his knowledge of panic disorder, knowing what it was but not how to treat it.

When I returned to work, it was even worse than before. I was constantly called in by the office manager and told, "You have a bad attitude." "You're too quiet." "You're too loud." "You talk too much." "You don't talk enough." "You're a complainer." "You can't do your job." "You use too much overtime to get your job done." And on and on and on. As I had been advised before, I was a "good girl" and kept my mouth shut. But every night as I left the office, I'd burst into tears and spend all evening crying.

The stress spilled over into my personal life as well. The worse things got at work, the more my panic attacks escalated and I started avoiding other things. First I stopped going on trips with my boyfriend. Then I became fearful of going to a movie theater ... then out to eat. My professional life was in shambles and my personal life shriveled up, too. I developed a disconcerting inability to stand in long lines at grocery stores or to write out a check. I began to just buy enough items with cash so I could use the express lane.

I was still treating with the HMO psychologist when in June of 1989, he suggested that I take a medical leave of absence from work due to stress. I talked to my supervisor and the office manager and was assured there would be no adverse repercussions. Those two weeks were heaven. I took my new puppy on long walks and spent long hours on the patio, soaking up the sun and a tape program of self-esteem. When I returned to work, all was quiet. Like magic, the harassment, ridicule and snide remarks just stopped.

A little more than a month later, on my 20 year anniversary with the law firm, I came to work expecting to receive the promised seniority bonus. Instead, I was called in by the office manager and unceremoniously fired. She threw some cardboard boxes at me and told me to clean out my desk and get out.

That was the beginning of the end for me. I applied for and received unemployment. I started sending out resumés, but I never made it to one interview. I'd set the appointment, but I couldn't walk out my front door.

After a couple of months, I was informed by the unemployment office that they were going to terminate me because I wasn't making enough effort to find a job. When I explained that I was having panic attacks, I was told that that was a medical problem and I should seek state disability.

My boyfriend (we had been seeing each other 12 years by then) got bored with pizzas and videos and sitting around my house. Even though supportive, I began to suspect he was having trouble with my panic attacks and inability to go places. I chose to deny it. Then his son dropped by on the same weekend my boyfriend had supposedly gone to Las Vegas with one of his male friends. What an earful I got. I heard all about the new woman in my boyfriend's life and what they did and when they did it and how they did it. I confronted my boyfriend when he returned and everything was made perfectly clear.

I had been abandoned once again. First, my parents, then my job, then my ability to leave the house, and lastly the love of my life. Eventually, the shock and numbness of these losses was replaced by anger and bitterness.

I filed a Worker's Compensation lawsuit against the law firm for stress-related illness and was considered filing a wrongful termination lawsuit as well. While trying to find a wrongful termination attorney, I found out about Social Security Disability and filled out the necessary paperwork. I subsequently dropped the wrongful termination suit but, looking back at how much I had come to loathe attorneys, I'm still amazed that I used them in the end to survive.

It took almost two years for both the lawsuit and Social Security Disability to kick in. By that time, I was on the brink of putting my home on the market. A friend made my mortgage payments until I could again.

I was just about at the end of my rope. I looked at my bottle of Xanax and thought how easy it would be to put myself out of my misery. I thought that maybe I had already died and just didn't know it and what I was experiencing was Hell.

I made the decision to concentrate on getting well. I saw psychologists, psychiatrists, and went through two self-help programs. They made me think and gave me valuable insights, but the panic attacks (although better controlled) continued.

My sister also suffers from panic attacks. She called me one day and told me about an article in a magazine she read about a newsletter for agoraphobics. What did I have to lose? I made an inquiry, was sent a sample copy, and it opened a door I never knew existed.

The newsletter (The Mountain Climber) offered a chance to write to others suffering from panic attacks and agoraphobia. I tentatively put out feelers and found a remarkable response from people just as hungry as me for support and knowledge. I have formed many close friendships with some of my pen pals, though I have never set eyes on them except through exchanged photographs. Out of everything—medications, therapists, reading self-help books and spending lots of money on self-help programs, my greatest source of strength and encouragement has come from the people I write. We share our successes and our not-so-good times (I refuse to see them as failures). We trade long distance hugs and hoorays. They are my extended family.

This brings me to the close of my story, but certainly not the end of it. In April of 1994, I was diagnosed with rheumatoid arthritis and find I have another battle to wage, this time on the physical front. In trying to confront my feelings about the arthritis, some old anger and bitterness has resurfaced.

My work on conquering the panic attacks has suffered a setback. However, I have also discovered some parallels between panic attacks and rheumatoid arthritis; they both offer their own kind of limitations, both are painful, one mentally and the other physically, and both require learning to accomplish and view things in a different way. My hope is that with two goals to focus on, I'll be twice as successful.

The country road outside Emily's house changed dramatically over the twenty years since she'd last left her home.

Who has Panic Disorder?

In the United States, two and a half to three million people (1.3-1.6 percent of the adult population) have or will have panic disorder at some time in their lives. They experience frequent, unprovoked panic attacks involving several symptoms. Women are affected twice as frequently as men.

Most people develop this disorder in their late teens or early twenties. Each year, new or recurrent panic disorder strikes more people than stroke, epilepsy, or AIDS.

Information provided by the National Institute of Mental Health (NIMH)

No More One of the Walking, Wounded, Living, Dead
by Dr. Marilyn Gellis

In 1976 I had my first panic attack. At that time, I had no idea what a panic attack was and certainly no idea what was happening to me.

I'd been to the dentist earlier that day and he'd given me a shot of Novocain before drilling my tooth. I then met some friends for dinner where I had a glass of wine and off we went to the movies.

Nothing exceptional was happening in my life, and although there were many stresses in my profession, I thought I was coping quite well.

Then, out of the clear blue sky, about halfway into the film, my hands became cold and clammy, my heart started to race, I became dizzy and nauseated and ran to the ladies room, where I threw up. The suddenness and severity of the attack was so devastating that I grabbed a cab from the theater (not even saying good-bye to my friends) and had the driver rush me to the nearest emergency room, sure that I was dying. After all emergency screening procedures proved normal, I was released and told to go home and rest.

As soon as I arrived home, I felt better and figured the Novocain must have reacted with the wine at dinner, and that was the cause of my distress. I resumed my normal daily activities with no further incidence.

About six months later, once again out of the blue, I had a second attack. This time it was at Disneyland. A friend had some Valium with her, so I took a half of a .5 mg. tablet, went to the first aid station, laid down for an hour and felt better. I just wanted to go home.

The next day I felt fine so I easily rationalized my feelings. They were caused by too much excitement, never seeing the connection between the two isolated incidents.

Then, on a Sunday in 1977, I was feeling a little anxious and stressed, so I decided to take a hot bath to help me relax. I crawled into bed to watch *60 Minutes* and started to feel very uneasy, weak, and uncomfortable. My palms started to sweat and I couldn't breathe. I had hot flashes, chest pains, and heart palpitations. A feeling of impending doom overwhelmed me and I was sure that I was having a heart attack.

I was afraid to drive and felt I couldn't wait for a taxi, so I rushed across the street to my neighbor's house and asked her to drive me to the emergency room where I was promptly admitted with a heart rate of 240 beats per minute. The doctors wanted to admit me to the hospital, but I refused. They kept me there for five hours until my heartbeat returned to normal. Then they sent me home after I promised to see my family physician the following morning. Once I returned home, I felt better. I was frightened, but experienced none of the physical and psychological terror of a few hours before, so I went to bed and slept quite well.

The following day, my doctor, finding nothing wrong with my EKG, diagnosed me as having tachycardia and prescribed Lanoxin (a heart medication) as a preventative measure. He said I had a bad case of "nerves" and suggested I take a few days off from work and try to relax.

After that Sunday's scare, my panic attacks became more frequent. I started making the rounds of different doctors. I was sure that I was dying but nobody believed me, since they could find nothing physically wrong. I had all of the routine lab tests, another EKG, a treadmill test, and blood chemistry work-ups. All results were in the normal ranges. Following my next panic attack, I seriously started doubting my doctor's diagnostic ability, so I made an appointment with the Chief Cardiologist at a neighboring hospital. Once again, he too found nothing physically wrong.

During one panic attack, my symptoms included dizziness, tingling and numbness of my arms. This time I was sure that I had a brain tumor, so I consulted a neurologist. I went through a whole different set of tests, studies, and scans yet had the same results ... normal!

My panic attacks were becoming more frequent and my symptoms were not always the same. A month later, when I once again experienced difficulty in breathing and feelings of suffocation, I wound up in the emergency room and all procedures proved normal once again.

I started listening in to all of my body symptoms and would catastrophize the slightest thing. When I had difficulty swallowing due to a tightness and lump in my throat, I arranged for a consultation with an Eye, Ear, Nose, and Throat Specialist. Another false alarm. Still no diagnosis.

One day a friend showed me an article in a women's magazine which described some of my symptoms and attributed them to Hypoglycemia, so off I rushed to an endocrinologist for an eight hour glucose tolerance test. Same normal results.

As a last resort, I went to a gastroenterologist when another when another well-meaning friend suggested my chest pains might be gas. I had an upper G.I. series which also proved normal and with each "normal" finding, I became more and more terrified. I knew something was seriously wrong with me, but no doctor could diagnose the problem.

All of my test results were returned to my original family practitioner who told me in no uncertain terms to "pull myself together" and I was nothing more than a hypochondriac and perhaps I should see a psychiatrist and stop wasting his time.

Due to the devastating effects of my unknown illness and the attacks which were occurring much more frequently, my perimeter got smaller and smaller. I became virtually paralyzed with irrational fears. Like the ripples of a stone dropped into a placid pool of water, my circle of fear spread out to encompass all areas of my life. From a creative, personable, vibrant, articulate extrovert, I turned into a recluse with millions of excuses as to why I couldn't attend any social functions, go to the market, drive, eat in restaurants, go to the movies, etc. I only felt safe and secure at home. I continually checked my door to make sure the paramedics could get in when called, and lifted the receiver to make sure the phone was working so I could call for help.

My main terror was the thought of mental illness, and now my own trusted physician was confirming my worst fears. Words like madness, insanity, crazy, and lunacy raced through my mind, evoking images of padded cells and straight jackets. I didn't want to live, yet I was too chicken to kill myself, so I reluctantly made an appointment with a psychiatrist. He prescribed antidepressants, but I rebelled against taking any medication. I had to be in complete control of my life and once I swallowed a pill, I had no control over the effect it would have on me. I panicked at the thought of the possible side effects. Although I fought taking the medication, I did keep my weekly appointments with my psychiatrist.

It was the blackest summer of my life. Each day my fears and depression worsened. I couldn't sleep. The only time I left my house was to visit the doctor. I couldn't concentrate. I'd try to read something and wound up reading the same sentence over and over again. Even though I had the money, I couldn't pay my bills. Everything was too much of an effort. I had no energy and all I did was cry.

Some people lose weight when they are depressed, others self-medicate with drugs and alcohol. My "drugs" were chocolate, caffeine, and nicotine. On the way back from the psychiatrist's office (which was the only place I went that summer) I traditionally stopped at the market to stock up on ice cream, candy, cigarettes, coffee, and dog food. (I had five dogs at the time and if not for them, I would have committed myself to a mental institution.) I gained forty pounds in two months. In addition to being an emotional basket case, I was a physical wreck as well. I had bottomed out. The only light I could see at the end of the tunnel was an oncoming train.

And then it happened. Since I didn't want to see or be seen by anyone during the day and couldn't sleep at night, I watered my outside plants in the middle of the night. I don't remember the exact date, but I'll never forget the experience.

On the left side of my house, next to the driveway, I had planted a cactus that a friend had discarded. It was a night blooming Cercus, and quite ugly and thorny. I never paid much attention to it and left it there since it required a minimum of care and served as a good deterrent to burglars.

On this particular night when I went to water it, I saw on it the most magnificent flower I had ever seen. I couldn't believe my eyes. This cactus that had never bloomed in the ten years I had it, amidst its ugliness and thorns, produced a flower that was complete perfection. I get chills even as I write this because that flower was a turning point in my life. When I saw such beauty could be produced and emerge from such ugliness, I realized from my deep despair that something, too, might be able to flourish. I cried that night as I have never cried before and then a calmness followed.

The next morning, I called a trusted friend and asked him to come over and sit with me while I took the medication my psychiatrist had prescribed six months ago that lay untouched in the medicine cabinet. I then made an appointment with my Rabbi to discuss my "condition," ask for his advice, and tell him about the "miracle" which had occurred in my life.

I have never been devoutly religious, but this cactus blooming, to me, was a sign ... a spiritual awakening. I was no longer alone ... there was a Higher Power. I just had to acknowledge it and let it in.

Even though I still didn't know what was wrong with me, the medication was beginning to lift my depression and block some of my anxiety. I became semi-functional and was able to return to work, but I still existed in a state of anticipatory anxiety ... not knowing when, where, or if the next attack would occur. I continued to avoid all other common places and activities.

Then another unexpected and unexplained development occurred. While watching television one night, I saw a program with an agoraphobic as its main character AND IT WAS ME! All my symptoms, all my fears, all my anxiety was portrayed on the screen and I finally had a name for my "condition." I wasn't alone! I wasn't going crazy. What I had was agoraphobia! My self-diagnosis in itself was therapeutic and offered my first ray of hope for potential recovery.

Life at its best is not easy, but I found that as soon as I gave up trying to control my life, the pieces started to fit together like a well-made puzzle, and things started falling into place.

I suffered from the devastation of agoraphobia and vowed if I ever became functional again, I would dedicate my life to helping others with this problem. This gave birth to the Institute for Phobic Awareness.

Because of problems (health, legal, etc.) with my school district, I had to take a year off from work. This gave me the opportunity to research and read everything and anything I could get my hands on regarding anxiety and panic-related disorders. It also afforded me the time to fly to New York to meet with Dr. Manny Zane and Dr. Donald Klein, two of the most respected authorities in the field of phobias and panic disorders, and to become more knowledgeable in current treatment modalities. Upon my return from Workman's Compensation leave, I was assigned to teach at a residential drug and alcohol recovery center in Desert Hot Springs. It was there that I became introduced to, and immersed myself in, the Twelve Step program of A.A. that I saw used so successfully in the recovery process of my students. This prompted me to start using the 12-step program for my own anxiety problems and I eventually founded Phobics Anonymous. That led me to writing "From Anxiety Addict to Serenity Seeker." I got stronger and stronger as I used the 12-step tools to rebuild my life.

I know I have to rid myself of my "what if" negative, pessimistic, catastrophic thinking. I also have my Bill of Rights.

BILL OF RIGHTS

1. I do not have to feel guilty just because someone else does not like what I do, say, think, or feel.

2. It is okay for me to feel angry and to express it in responsible ways.

3. I do not have to assume full responsibility for making decisions, particularly where others share responsibility for making the decision.

4. I have the right to say "I don't understand" without feeling stupid or guilty.

5. I have the right to say "I don't know." I have the right to say "no" without feeling guilty. I do not have to apologize or give reasons when I say no.

6. I have the right to ask others to do things for me and I have the right to refuse requests which others make of me.

7. I have the right to tell others when I think they are manipulating, conning, or treating me unfairly.

8. I have the right to refuse additional responsibilities without feeling guilty.

9. I have the right to tell others when their behavior annoys me.

10. I do not have to compromise my personal integrity.

11. I have the right to make mistakes and to be responsible for them. I have the right to be wrong.

12. I do not have to be liked, admired, or respected by everyone for everything I do.

My "Shoulda" "Woulda" "Coulda" thinking only leads to FRUSTRATION

F ear of people, places, and things
R etreating to my "safe place"
U nconditional surrender to my fears
S eeking excuses
T raitor to myself
R esignation and resentments
A nxiety and agitation
T error, instead of tranquillity
I nadequacy and low self esteem
O ppression and obsessive thoughts
N egative feelings

I also know that I must live in the present, one day at a time. In order to prevent a setback I must avoid:

1. **Exhaustion** - I can't allow myself to become overly tired or in poor health caused by work addictions, compulsive overeating, or taking on responsibilities that really belong to someone else. Good health and enough rest are important. When I feel well, I am more apt to think well.

2. **Dishonesty** - This begins with a pattern of unnecessary little lies and deceits with fellow workers, friends, and family. Then come important lies to myself. Rationalizing, making excuses for not doing what I do not want to do, or for doing what I know I should not do.

3. **Impatience** - Things are not happening fast enough. Or, others are not doing what they should or what I want them to do.

4. **Argumentativeness** - Arguing small and ridiculous points of view may be a sign that I am not dealing with my real issue. Arguing over and over indicates a need to be right, and an effort to control. I must be alert for "If I could just make you understand."

5. **Depression** - Unreasonable or unaccountable despair may occur in cycles and should be dealt with and talked about. Depression may be an indication that I have been stuffing feelings. Talking is one tool of recovery.

6. **Frustration** - We may feel frustrated at people or at situations in general that don't seem to be going "right." Everything is not going to be the way I want it or think it should be.

7. **Self-Pity** - "Why do these things happen to me?" "Nobody appreciates all that I am doing (for them)." "Things would be better if only ... " I always have choices. Self-pity indicates blaming outside circumstances.

8. **Cockiness** - "I've got it made. I can handle it. It will never again happen to me." This is dangerous thinking. I must continually remember most relapses occur when I let up on my own recovery program.

9. **Expecting too much from others** - "I've changed; why hasn't everyone else?" It's an extra plus if they do, but I cannot expect others to change their lifestyle just because I have. The only changes I can make are with myself.

10. **Letting up on the discipline** - Of prayer, meditation, daily inventory, because of complacency or boredom. I cannot afford to be bored with my program. The cost of a setback is always too great.

11. **Wanting too much** - Perhaps we're in a hurry to make up for lost time. I do not set goals and I expect too much. "Happiness is not having what you want, but wanting what you have."

12. **Forgetting gratitude** - That's when I look negatively at my life, concentrating on problems that still are not totally corrected. It's good to remember where I started and how much better life is now.

13. **Protecting** - Remember I am responsible for myself and others are responsible for themselves.

14. **Powerlessness and Unmanageability** - Admitting and accepting are the cornerstones of recovery. I apply this to my life on a daily basis. I go to meetings, learn to work the steps and TALK ABOUT WHAT'S REALLY GOING ON WITH ME.

I find the best way to deal with my problem is with Acceptance. It is the answer to all my problems today. When I am disturbed, it is because I find some person, place, thing, or situation, some fact of my life unacceptable to me and I can find no serenity until I accept that person, place, thing, or situation as being exactly the way it is supposed to be at this moment. Nothing, absolutely nothing, happens in God's world by mistake. Unless I accept life completely on life's terms, I cannot be happy. I need to concentrate not so much on what needs to be changed in the world as on what needs to be changed in me and in my attitudes.

I believe it is my duty to myself to develop a well rounded life using the abilities which I possess within myself.

1. I shall do something today about my health, my figure, my appearance, my voice and my speech.

2. I shall learn something today because I believe in personal growth.

3. I shall employ the light touch today and bring joy and laughter to at least one person.

4. I shall use gracious ways today in my contact with others.

5. I shall develop my senses a little today in the appreciation of beauty.

6. I shall have faith today in the great creative force and realize that I am an important part of a great play.

7. I shall live serenely and free of fear today.

12 WAYS TO ACCEPT

1. ACCEPT, that I am a phobic, and need help and that help can be found by attending Phobics Anonymous meetings, reading literature, taking medication if necessary, and by practicing the 12 step program at all times.

2. ACCEPT, that I am powerless over anyone, but that I have the power to change myself.

3. ACCEPT, that I am not responsible for anyone's actions, but I am responsible to myself.

4. ACCEPT, God or a Higher Power back into my life, to LET GO AND LET GOD. To learn to have patience by not taking things back too quickly and trying to manage or play God myself.

5. ACCEPT, that I am a good person and it is OK to be good to myself. Don't be afraid to be happy and enjoy what is beautiful. Always remember, I'M OK, GOD DOESN'T MAKE JUNK.

6. ACCEPT, tolerance with others and especially myself, having faith that can grow in our P.A. program, and become a whole person again.

7. ACCEPT, things I do not like, realizing that all things do not have to be good to be acceptable. By having to let someone we love suffer for their own mistakes, or actions, by detaching with love.

8. ACCEPT, that I do not have to be right all the time and that it is OK to be wrong or make a mistake. Our mistakes can be a learning experience.

9. ACCEPT, that it is OK to say I'm wrong and ask forgiveness when I hurt or wrong someone.

10. ACCEPT, that I must be open-minded enough to listen thoughtfully to the opinions of others.

11. ACCEPT, that each day is a new beginning. It is within my power to make that day as good and happy as I want it to be.

12. ACCEPT, that I have no control over the PAST and that TOMORROW is beyond my immediate control for it is yet unborn. This leaves only TODAY. Let me therefore live but ONE DAY AT A TIME. If I can just follow the motto:

Live for today - Dream for Tomorrow

Learn from Yesterday.

I know I will stay on the right track, and last but not least, I know I must learn to trust myself to know what's best for me, to have complete trust in my ability to determine my own needs. My role is to fully express myself. Today I embrace every opportunity to be who I am. I am not ashamed of my needs.

I am a unique and special individual and my needs are a positive extension of my personhood. There are those who feel they know what is best for me and there are others who tell me what my needs are; I thank them, but I listen to my inner voice. I determine my choices and needs and the directions I'll take in recovery. Today I am willing to take time to listen to myself. Today I make a conscious decision to trust my inner voice and fulfill my needs. I must remember that even the great cathedrals are built just one brick at a time. Easy Does It!

Anyone interested in obtaining information on Phobics Anonymous or interested in locating or starting a chapter in their area, please send a self-addressed stamped envelope to :

Phobics Anonymous World Service Headquarters
P.O. Box 1180
Palm Springs, CA 92263

Any small donation to cover printing and handling costs would be greatly appreciated, but not mandatory.

All I Thought I Had to Do Was Love
by Ricardo Vicente Reyes

Panic disorder and agoraphobia have been a blessing and a scourge for me. From this experience of acute suffering and mental pain I have received enlightenment, self-knowledge, and a small stream of light which falls through the darkness; my hope. At times it is like a small flame on the wall of my house, like a sparkle left as the sun is setting a dark room.

I was born in Los Angeles in the turbulence of a dysfunctional family tormented by alcoholism. My stepfather, the drunk, was the perpetrator of violence and sorrow in my young life.

My mother, in her hopeless, loveless relationship turned her rage on the two children she had given birth to from previous relationships that had failed. I was the second child born to her. At age three or four this mother who I adored tried to burn me with a flaming coil of newspaper. She was punishing me for playing with fire. It was there that terror, not fear, found itself firmly planted in my little child's mind.

I began to act out at the age of four or five. My mother took me into the busy streets and stores of downtown Los Angeles. When I'd look up at the skyscrapers, I feared their falling upon me. I was a little boy terrified of the streetcars, escalators, and elevators. My mother's method of dealing with this rebellious behavior was to beat me violently in public. She'd drag me by the arm as I'd become limp with terror on the escalator stairs. I was sure they were going to swallow me up.

Every experience that involved machines caused me to panic, and every episode of panic resulted in the same treatment; violence followed by verbal abuse. My mother called me a "sissy," a "little girl," a "cry baby," a "faggot." But all the beatings and verbal abuse didn't take away the fear.

At home, too, I felt increasingly less safe. My mother's divorce left her full of rage that she directed at me. Of all five children, I was the most sensitive. (Not the weakest.) I became the constant victim of her brutality. I was whipped, beaten daily, slugged, kicked, mocked, and humiliated. There was no affection, love, or caring.

At the age of eight I was raped by a barber in his shop. My mother had left me with him. I became even more afraid of men. When my mother returned, all my dark eyes could say to her was, "How could you abandon me to this monster?" By thirteen, I was not only a victim of her terror, but had to deal with memories.

I became sexually mature and my identity led to the realization that I was a homosexual youth. More molestations and one violent rape that almost led to my death followed. This only added to my mother's ammunition. I became the scapegoat, disappointing my Latino mother. I was a perverted person, a son to repudiate. My mother began collecting weapons to discipline my rebellious nature. (This included a horse whip.) I was a strong child and had a mind of my own. Thank God! But I lived in constant fear as my mother was a time bomb. I eventually was taken to an institution after a brutal beating. My leg was nearly broken.

At age 19, I was mentally shattered by things I couldn't understand and slipped into my first depression. I had nightmares of being murdered by men.

I was afraid to be alone, afraid to leave my apartment. I couldn't be in markets; the lights bothered me. These problems were but a glimpse of things to come. In the meantime, therapy and my own exploration of painting and writing allowed me to transcend the mental anguish of those confused thoughts. The anxiety went away for a very long time.

I was 30 years old when I suddenly felt trapped on a crowded Los Angeles freeway. I became extremely fearful and I wanted out NOW. These feelings went on for years and I received no help.

In 1985, I fell while on a bus in San Francisco. This seemingly unimportant event led me tumbling down a rabbit hole. Within minutes I was hiding and shaking, screaming and crying with terror. I couldn't explain then what was happening to me, but now I know I was having my first real panic attack. I didn't leave the house for four days. When I did try to leave, I had to hold onto the sides of the buildings to remain standing. My partner at the time watched with utter disbelief. Two days later I was told by a psychologist that I was agoraphobic. I was introduced to Xanax and put into a treatment program.

I was afraid to ride the bus alone to work. I lived in fear of strange things like wetting my pants. I was under acute stress all the time, but I coped. It took me more than a year and a half to function fairly normally, but leaving the city was really frightening.

My link to this illness never left me. I felt it hiding underneath me like a ghost, ready to leap. But I continued on. Soon the anxiety and agoraphobia were like memories again.

Each time I had a crisis, it was preceded by a series of deep depressions. These depressions were often caused by serious experiences that exposed my vulnerability; the ending of love relationships, job related stresses, deaths of friends, violent acts by lovers, and hate-crimes against me by my students.

I have been a high school teacher for many years, working at both academic and continuation schools for dropouts and at-risk youth. I was victimized far too many times by both students and faculty members because I am a homosexual man. But I always felt powerless in dealing with my abusers. I tried to get help but nobody wanted to deal with me. Even well-meaning people would not put their necks out. My principal told me his concern was to protect the students, even if they were abusing me. The counselor, who was gay, felt too concerned about how he might look. The police told me I had to be attacked physically before they could intervene. These events happened at a very excellent public school in San Francisco.

I ran away from that city in 1990 and returned to Los Angeles only to find myself in the same mess again. A break up with my lover of five years depressed me, but I didn't feel the symptoms of panic disorder or agoraphobia. Even though I had one tragedy after another, nothing let out that ghost looming inside me.

Two years later, I began experiencing anxiety again. I first noticed dizzy spells. Then one day while teaching, I began to

"Mesh. Steals of Dreams" *by Ricardo V. Reyes*
(pen and ink) from the book The Dreamers

de-personalize. I felt I was in a tunnel, visually leaving the room. I began hyperventilating. Twenty minutes later, I was in an emergency hospital bed, crying and shaking and full of terror. I was tranquilized and sent home.

My condition worsened. In March of 1993, I was walking to work to start a new job. I suddenly froze in my tracks, unable to move. I panicked. I hyperventilated. I nearly crawled back to my apartment. Within two hours I was in a psychiatric hospital and remained there for nine days. I'd never experienced such terror. I couldn't go out. I couldn't walk down the street. I couldn't go into markets. I couldn't visit clubs I frequented. I became increasingly homebound.

I stayed ill, floating through many months of problematic quests for help I didn't receive. I didn't understand why I was ill; I couldn't see the real issues. I saw therapists and psychiatrists who put me on drugs and tried various therapies, but none of these therapists seemed to understand the problem of agoraphobia and how to treat it. Talking about my traumas was clearly not the answer. Every drug I tried made me very sick. Nonetheless, I began using Xanax as a tranquilizer with increased frequency.

In 1994, I'd experienced bouts of panic attacks and deep depression for several months. I crawled through life and felt hopeless, but I did not give up. I tried various doctors. Then one day, while eating breakfast in a restaurant, I began feeling an especially strange and extreme sensation of unsettling anxiety. Terror overcame me. I managed to get myself to a hospital and was again put into a psychiatric hospital, only to repeat that same useless process of drug therapy. I never received what I really needed.

After this hospitalization, I began developing social phobias including the fear of people. I couldn't concentrate on conversations and had attacks when company was due to arrive at my home.

With great disappointment, I learned that my home was not really safe. On three occasions, I've had such severe panic attacks that I've called 911 for an ambulance.

R.V.Reyes 12-75

"Our Lady of Guadalupe" *by Ricardo V. Reyes (mixed media)*

A program called Chaange was referred to me by a friend in 1994. That was the road to the light. I saw hope where there hadn't been any before.

In attempting to reach my recovery, I have had to often do the unexpected or that very thing which I most feared. Many times the decision to change my pattern of agoraphobic avoidance behavior has come about by making a spontaneous decision.

I recently made such a move. I left Los Angeles and traveled about 100 miles away from home and totally out of my geographic safety zone. I had anxiety, but my excitement overrode my fears. I allowed myself to break away.

I was moderately calm the entire two days and nights I was gone. I remained calm on the way home. This feeling stayed with me until the morning when I experienced the old feelings again, but I later felt very calm and broke my routine of running home. I visited a restaurant I have never eaten in and I went to a friend's house I had not visited in months. By breaking my long agoraphobic pattern one day, I received a gift in the form of some serenity the following day. I gained some self-confidence and even forgot for a few hours what it felt like to be sick.

Some of the lessons I've learned have involved old patterns of behavior and thinking. I've learned about toxic codependence. I've begun to root out those people who do not support me, but instead use guilt to manipulate me.

I am going through this long, painful process towards recovery, thanks to tools I've learned. And I see that I discover something new about myself with each crisis I face. A recent experience taught me something I'd never thought about; as a child and adolescent, I was the virtual prisoner of my mother's control. It occurred to me that I am not that little child anymore. I'm an adult and I can make decisions that can change the course of my life.

I took a good hard look at my job working with at risk dropout students, many who are gang members. Most have given up on life and are not unlike my own family, Latino and very poor. For years I felt the commitment to work with these kinds of students, but recently began to realize that I was getting ill because of all the baggage I had to deal with in relationship to them.

I felt like that powerless little boy I used to be, unable to decide my destiny and trapped in the prison created by my mother. My panic attacks became worse with each month that passed. I finally realized that I have the choice to do something else; I have power regarding my present situation and my future. I saw that quitting my job could change my life. No matter what the consequences, this could help me gain back my health. Such control over my life is what I feel committed to now, as it holds the key to my recovery.

This theme of my little boy taking over and making decisions, reacting, and responding, has been a problem all my adult life. I did not realize how difficult my life had become because the adult me had stepped aside to permit the child to take over. This child running my life has been a scared, scarred, and terrified individual, holding the memories of my torture, rapes, and abuse.

I've come to acknowledge that this little boy within me is good and always has been wonderful. However, because he is full of fear, I must stop him from running my life so I can rid myself of the panic lingering within me, waiting to strike unannounced. I must comfort and reassure him that I will be his protector from now on.

I've had many childlike attitudes. My little child expected everyone in the world to be good, honest, and to love him unconditionally. (Isn't that how children start off thinking? Isn't that part of our innocence?) I gave love unconditionally, believing that all I had to do was love others in order to be lovable and loved. Now I know that it's my little child *and my adult self I need to love unconditionally.* In loving myself, I will learn how to love others in a healthy way.

I've also learned that the dangerous world I feared so much as a child is *inside* and not *outside* of me. Once I create a peaceful and safe place within me, my internal chaos and terror will be replaced with a safer world for me to live in.

Editor's Note: Ricardo is also a very accomplished artist, which he didn't mention in his story.

Searching
by Brenda M. Rivet

I am a wife, mother, and grandmother. The past forty years haven't been easy, especially when accompanied by panic attacks and agoraphobia. But I've sure had one learning experience after another.

Beginning years ago and for many years after, I was confused about the awful physical symptoms I experienced for no apparent reason. I'd get sweaty hands, a pounding heart, weak legs, and my mind would race. I just wanted to run. This would happen at school, stores, restaurants, and even at home. Just getting up, going to bed, eating, dressing, and little chores took everything out of me. I eventually became housebound for awhile. Why did these things happen? I didn't know, but I didn't think I could be the only one who had this problem. Someone had to know what this "thing" was. So I searched for answers.

I didn't let panic attacks stop me from doing everything I wanted, but dating certainly wasn't easy with such symptoms lingering over my shoulders all the time. When I met Ray, he seemed different than other men I'd met. I hid my anxiety from him the best I could and for as long as I was able to. I made up excuses why I couldn't go to the movies or to a restaurant, saying I was tired or didn't feel well. But after many excuses I had to tell him the truth. And without the answers we fell in love and married, bonding our search together.

I had little anxiety from pregnancy. Having to go to the hospital is what I feared! When my boys decided to enter this world, however, I welcomed them with open arms. Ray stayed with me the entire time I was in the hospital and that's when fathers weren't even allowed in the delivery room. I didn't want my sons to go through what I had all those years, so I looked for answers more than ever.

I wanted to become a hairdresser, so getting through hairdressing school became a goal. It made me very anxious but I dealt with aspects of being there by making myself more comfortable. For example, it didn't feel safe on a bus, so I got a ride from a friend instead.

I sure didn't want to go to school the day I had to take my boards, but Ray pushed me a bit and my friend from school came along. I learned that a glass of water is a friend as well. I passed the boards and was elated.

Up to this point I'd prayed and white-knuckled through everything I did. I'd gone to doctor after doctor before finding one who knew what I had. He gave me medication and I started behavioral therapy. I finally began to understand what was going on with me.

I found out about a support group and met people like me. How refreshing to sit in a room with others who actually knew how I felt! These people didn't get strange looks on their faces when hearing a person couldn't stay alone or go out to eat.

Books and newsletters relating to anxiety disorders were important to my recovery, also. I learned about a ten week program and although it wasn't a close drive, I figured it'd be worth it. I believed the people there would help make my next ride to the meeting easier and I was right. I finished the ten week program with much more knowledge about panic attacks, agoraphobia, and behavioral therapy.

All these things were stepping stones. But perhaps the biggest one I crossed was when I began to believe in myself. Once crossing that boulder, it seemed there wasn't anything I couldn't do. For example, I'd seen the same doctor for ten years and felt we were at a stalemate. I went neither forward nor backward. I wanted off my medication. With my newfound confidence, I confronted my doctor with how I felt. He was taken aback and gave me excuses why I wasn't pushing ahead and told me why it wasn't a good time to get off the medication. But *I* believed it was a good time; I felt I needed a new approach in order to move on. So I searched for another doctor.

There's been much hard work, but I encourage anyone who suffers from agoraphobia or panic attacks to never give up searching for your answers. If one therapy doesn't work, try another. The same goes for medication, doctors, and even books. Believe me, there is an answer out there for you. It might be different for you than for me or someone else, but it is there. Above all, always remember to believe in yourself and there won't be anything you can't do.

For so many years I was lost and confused, but confusion has been replaced with knowledge. Everything that used to be an effort is now done with little to no effort. And being housebound is but a memory.

I dedicate this story to my granddaughter, Deonna. I am proud to say when she was born, I was able to see her in the hospital with all the anxiety of a new grandparent.

What causes Panic Disorder?

Research suggests there are both biological and psychological components which interact. Family and twin studies indicate that panic disorder involves some genetic vulnerability.

Studies suggest that people with panic disorder have a low tolerance for the body's normal physiological and psychological response to stress; their body's alarm response goes off with little or no provocation.

Some researchers theorize that the disturbance in coping mechanisms is a product of repeated life stresses in predisposed individuals, eventually leading to panic disorder.

Research also suggests that people with panic disorder may not be able to utilize the body's own naturally produced anxiety-reducing substances. It may be that the neuronal receptors that bind with these substances are abnormal in people with panic disorder.

Information provided by the National Institute of Mental Health (NIMH)

Trying Hard to Find
that Panda I Deserve
by Susan Cerny Park aka Princess Bonessa Vox

Editor's Note: This story concentrates on social anxiety disorder, similar in ways to agoraphobia, yet different in others. Because of similarities and because many people with panic disorder and/or agoraphobia may also suffer from social anxiety disorder, I've included this story. I think it will be helpful and insightful to many.

I am a 26 year old woman of mixed heritage; European and Korean. I've been diagnosed with social anxiety disorder, chronic depression, and obsessive compulsive disorder. It is difficult for me to write about my life and all the pain I've gone through, but I want to share my story in hopes of helping others.

Social anxiety disorder in its severe form is incapacitating. People with this problem do not want to be the object of attention, so the greater the number of people I am around, the worse are my anxiety symptoms: stomach butterflies doing a slam dance, accelerated pulse, confusion, muscle incoordination, a feeling of dread when I need to perform, and a great fear of the unknown.

I believe SAD is worsened and perpetuated by shame and humiliation encountered early in life, and believe me, I've experienced a lot of that.

I've been very nervous around people, especially men, for as long as I can remember. Even as a baby, I was very quiet. There was unhappiness in my home and my father beat my mother on three occasions. He was verbally abusive to me, calling me stupid, ugly, scrawny, chopsticks, and meatless. For some reason, he didn't do this to my older sister. When he'd say these things, my mother would give my father a look to apologize to me, but he wouldn't. She'd then take me into the bathroom and comfort me.

Despite this, I was relatively happy until I began school. What a nightmare! I was so quiet that the teachers told my mother I needed to go to a school for slightly retarded children! My mother would not let them do that, and once the teachers saw my grades, they changed their minds. I was put in a slower-paced class that was somewhat more comfortable for me as the children weren't as pushy.

My first grade teacher, Mrs. Smithson, was very kind and understanding. But I couldn't stand playing ridiculous games like Duck Chase. One kid would hit another's head, then that child had to run and be chased around the ring until they could find a spot to sit down. I couldn't run fast, so the boys always picked me.

I told another teacher that this wasn't a game or a way of playing. She told me to either participate or go inside and write. I told her I'd be glad to write, at which point she made me "play" that "game" again. On another occasion I was hit in the head with a basketball. I remember hearing kids laughing at me.

I don't feel especially good about my heritage. A big reason for that is from the racial slurring and badgering I've received. In school, Caucasian boys often made fun of me by making their "roundeyes" look slanted and speaking in some mock Asian tongue. And I recall how in the first grade, the other children boasted of their father's names one day. I proudly said my father's name was Yong Sook. The children laughed in a mean, vicious manner. To me, that felt like the beginning of the end. I realized I was a minority.

At six and a half, my parents got divorced. It was a blessing. My father turned out to be the stupid one because he lost three daughters and a very brilliant and remarkable wife. We'd lived in Maryland, but after the divorce I moved with my mother and sisters to a college town in Mississippi. Talk about culture shock! The city is known for its hospitality, but beneath that facade lies a coven of small minds and prejudice. And the school system didn't help.

Most of the children were Caucasian and Afro-American. I stuck out like a green thumb; none of the kids looked like me. Not being used to seeing any Asians, these children called me just about every derogatory name one might call someone of a minority nationality; Jap, Gook, Chink, Nigger, Pocahontas. Just as in Maryland, these kids made fun of my eyes and screamed out sounds they made to imitate an Asian language. I was reminded by those kids that I live in white America.

Some of the teachers also made fun of me and my ethnic background. Some made a point of it to tell the class that "Susan Park is shy." I'd go for days without saying a word except for "Present." Reading out my grades, which were always good, caused even more of a barrier between myself and the others. Early peer rejection is bad for everyone, but a person with social anxiety disorder can be devastated by it. It was impossible to make any friends. Through all those years of schooling I didn't have a friend. Not one. Even the so-called "nerds" had their group and I didn't fit with them, either. It's been hard to realize how mean kids can be.

In the fourth grade I had a teacher who yelled at me, "Don't you know how to understand American money?!!!" I cried while a white boy laughed at me. I was too afraid to tell my mother, being raised on fear and guilt.

I had problems on the school bus, too. Kids would stretch out their legs so I couldn't sit next to them. One day I got fed up and pushed a boy's legs out of the way. He proceeded to cuss me out for five minutes. Then he moved. I've thought often of what Rosa Parks did in Alabama; one day she stopped sitting in the back of the bus and set the world on fire. Maybe that's why some people here call me Susan *Parks*!

I was 17 years old in 1986 when I sought counseling at a state-funded mental health clinic. The counselors didn't seem trained to help people with severe long-term problems. One "counselor" told me to "bake a cake, take a hot bath, and just smile more!"

I did have one very sharp counselor who really cared. Through him I saw how inadequate the others were. I've continued going there because I can see the psychiatrist who prescribes my medications. Sometimes, especially with the newer class of antidepressants, a paradoxical effect happens in which these drugs make me more depressed. I'm currently on Klonopin, but

I've been prescribed a multitude of medications including Limbitrol, Sinequan, Tofranil, Norpramine, Luvox, Effexor, Prozac, Anafranil, Zoloft, and Wellbutrin. Klonopin has killed my appetite and I'm only 94 pounds as it is, but it is the only drug that has helped my concurrent depression of 26 years of anxiety and nervousness. I'm grateful it exists.

I've been concerned that some psychiatrists push drugs so much that patients end up being treated more like medical guinea pigs without much concern to the side effects. I think doctors need to give out love and compassion and not overprescribe pills.

I've tried alternative therapies, also, but have not found them helpful. In fact, I've noticed feeling more depressed after listening to subliminal tapes, a tool that has possibly helped others.

In the summer of 1992, I was in Canada, staying with a sister in British Columbia. It was there that I read books on self help and East-Indian health practices. I also saw four psychics and learned to meditate after being advised by one that meditation would help with my nervousness and overproduction of adrenaline. My older sister had taken a Transcendental Meditation class with no adverse reactions, so I didn't think twice about doing it. I didn't think about my sister not having chemical imbalances, however.

On July 23, I woke up at 2:30 a.m. and felt depressed. The sensations worsened by the minute, becoming unbearable, as if the left and right hemispheres of my brain were merging into one. I felt I was going to have a break with reality and wanted to black out. I wanted to be dead because nothing, not even death, could be worse than what I was experiencing. I'd experienced the agony of a kidney stone in 1986 which made me feel I was being stabbed to death. The pain of this night was worse than even that.

By 4:00 a.m. I was screaming uncontrollably for my sister to take me to the nearest hospital. I waited for what seemed like forever in the Emergency Room before a doctor told me I was having a panic attack and that I was not depressed because I was too nervous to be depressed! He prescribed Serax, irritated that I didn't agree with his diagnosis. "Look," he said. "I've been a doctor for 18 years. I'm right about this. You're not depressed!" I went back to my sister's apartment and took the Serax.

Not long after, I woke up again feeling out of control and as if I'd reached a bottomless pit. I called an ambulance. A police officer escorted me instead. The ambulance never came.

My sister and I were "greeted" by a nurse. "We're too busy here," she told the officer. People stared at me as I cried and yelled out in pain. "Susan, keep it down," the nurse said. "You're disturbing the other patients!"

The diagnosis of the second doctor was the same as the first. He prescribed Haldol, an anti-epileptic and anti-psychotic drug. Back at the apartment my pain was so severe I was convinced it was a kidney stone. I returned to another hospital, doubled-over in emotional pain, terror, and panic. I went numb and yelled so loudly that a group of apparent internists stood in the hall, looking baffled. That's all they did.

After an X ray proved negative for a kidney stone, I was sent to a social worker. I went home again and fell asleep. But the next day I had an epileptic seizure from the Haldol. The doctor hadn't told me to take another pill to offset that possibility. It was later that I realized that I, indeed, had suffered from severe panic attacks that night, along with suicidal depression.

The next two weeks I experienced minor panic attacks alternating with sudden depression. I was terrified to go to sleep for fear the monster would come again in the night.

I went to a mental health center because I was told I could get free medication and great help. I soon discovered I was in a stabilization unit for schizophrenics. I was asked several questions like "Don't you have any friends?" "Didn't you do normal activities in school?" "Didn't you date?" The Jekyll and Hyde director smiled sweetly. "Why can't you be like your sister here with the Master's Degree?" she snapped. Her fire-eater statements caused me to break down and cry.

I believe that this entire sordid experience on the 23rd was related to the sudden euphoria I'd experienced on July 4th. Meditation had made me feel I'd made contact with a Supreme Being and for the first time in my life I felt as though my past was completely erased. It was a high that had lasted about one and a half hours. In retrospect, I feel I was one of those rare cases to have an adverse reaction to something designed to help. The depression I believe was caused by that experience was so painful that I would have gladly taken cyanide or put a gun to my head had I had those resources. Maybe I didn't because I am strong, despite everything.

After this experience, I felt rage toward my father, thinking of the repeated damaging statements he'd made to me as a young child. I wrote him that he owed me money for all the medications and counseling I've had because of him. He responded by mailing my mother a letter stating that all my problems were her fault. I know he will never change. But I must.

In 1986, I tried a self help program for agoraphobia. It didn't help me at all with my inherent social anxiety, but it did touch on generalized anxiety and cognitive restructuring.

I've learned and used desensitization techniques such as repeatedly facing a fear, but it only helped so far. I also attempted flooding (staying in the fearful situation no matter how fearful I get) and making a hierarchy of social activities from least to most severe, working myself up. But I'd get to a certain level and then go no further or even backtrack.

Therapy has done me little good and there are no therapists here that specialize in Social Anxiety Disorder . I've had to read up on this condition so much to help myself that I know a lot more than many therapists. Some counselors sigh when I use technical words because, I think, they feel insecure with the "patient" knowing more than they do. I've yet to see a therapist who knows what I am talking about.

I suggest people to keep shopping for a better therapist if disappointed with who you're with. Listen to talk radio shows where people call in to doctors for help. A lot of time you can get more help from people who have walked in your shoes than from therapists who don't understand.

There are tools I encourage others to give a chance, although they've not worked for me: repeating positive affirmations and listening to subliminal tapes.

After listening to them, I've gotten nightmares and also depressed. I believe the subconscious mind is "sub" for a damn good reason, but just because these two techniques did not work for me, I know they have helped others; everyone is like a thumbprint .... we're all individuals. I've lifted myself up by changing what I say to myself. I tell myself that I have a chemical imbalance, a no-fault brain disease so to speak. "Look," I say, "these status-quo people have not had your life or problems. And who knows what you will be doing in the future, even though you have a tendency to do things backwards naturally. In the long run, it just might pay off as a form of brilliance in an unconventional way like a light bulb going off."

If people give me a quizzical look or one that I'm half-baked (when I try to be humorous and they call me weird) I remind myself of the town I am in and tell myself there is nothing wrong with me. Or I tell myself that these people did not get enough love in their lives and are projecting their pathology onto me ... or that they are basically ignorant and they need to change their attitude toward phobics, or at least be willing to listen. And if they don't, then kill them with kindness. This is difficult, and I realize that looking back in the past is a strong habit, so I force myself to stay in the "great eternal now" and not waste anymore time looking back when I can use that time realizing my potential before this one life ends.

Another thing I tell myself is that even though I have anxiety symptoms every day, it is not every second of every day. I try to figure out what exactly makes my "fear button" light up and what relaxes me.

Throughout my day, I interject a lot of humor to lighten up the dark cloud. Humor also is an icebreaker for having to converse with people. For instance, sometimes the tension in a social encounter is so thick that I feel I need a strong tool to cut through it. What I do at these times is visualize a machete like the kind needed to cut the bamboo in my backyard. Then, lo and behold, an exotic, friendly giant panda is there waiting! (I have a big stuffed Panda named "Tub-Tub.")

A practical tool I've learned is to look at the eyebrows of those I'm speaking to and not at their eyes. If that's too difficult, one can try making eye contact with an animal and build from there. Focusing on a wall can also be helpful.

Sometimes I try to think up positive thoughts and build them up from there, maybe to an extreme, to counterbalance the negative thoughts in my mind and what I hear from others. I try to look at the simple joys of everyday life. I look at my daily planner and even if I've had another bad day, I try to find one uplifting or funny thing that happened. If I try to turn my thinking around bit by bit and it still isn't positive, I often end up with something from my day that was at least interesting and innovative.

Many self-conscious people tend to think the world revolves around them, that everybody is looking at or paying attention to them. When I'm tempted to do this, I say to myself, "The world does not revolve around me; I revolve around the world." Instead of "As the World Turns," it's "As Susan Turns," like a soap opera, where a mundane plot can go on and on but eventually resolves and ends.

I've begun a Taekwondo class. The instructor recently told me something that has stayed on my mind. "Susan," he said, "try not to dwell on negative happenings. It might help if you think of any good thing that happened in your day and focus on that instead. Then maybe better things will happen and those bad things won't seem so bad."

I think there needs to be a tape program on social phobia. Social anxiety disorder is not a simple phobia and is often hidden by agoraphobia. But social/anxiety is a growing phenomenon.

Most books on social anxiety disorder focus on what causes it, how society creates and perpetuates it, what it is, and it's history. In my experience, little is actually written about what one can do to help themself or get help. I wish there were more written about techniques, what to do or say in specific situations, and what to do when a dozen counselors, therapists, and doctors cannot help. This is not to discourage anyone from reading any of these books. By all means do, because they can help people who are not in the most severe stage of the phobia. The one book that has helped me out in the world is *Beyond Shyness* by Jonathan Berent.

I've learned from this condition that many people have several layers of insincerity to them, where one has to dig and dig to get to something real. A lot of people seem to learn early on how to make friends and to make it in this society by copying the behaviors of others. I think that in a sense, many people become clones of others. I've done the opposite. I wasn't an ultra-conformist because I am an individualist. Despite my fears, I've been strong and resistant to molding myself into who others appear to be.

Being socially disabled has limited my life. I went from having no friends in school, to no friends in college, to none at a Junior College, to none when I worked full-time. If I'd had better social skills (the art of small talk) maybe I would have made one or more friends in my age group. This condition has preempted me from finishing my degree, from many job opportunities (because most jobs require the ability to deal with the public), and a normal social life. I've felt trapped and controlled by my problem, although I am working hard on taking more control of my life and becoming more in command of situations.

I would like very much to move away from the town I live in, but I am impeded because driving out of town is still difficult for me. I get very confused. But I need to go where I can get help and where people are more open-minded.

It seems my progress is so slow and that my life is passing me by, but I am working at getting healthier. Because part of my brain has been stepped on so many times, I have decided to not let myself be treated like a doormat anymore. I am learning how to stick up for myself. It's frustrating and discouraging when I put a lot of mental and behavioral work into helping myself and then see someone who is less severely affected start to fly, but I'm moving steadily. I want to win the race, but if I don't, then I will be glad just to cross that line called life. The fact that I'm still alive tells me I have a lot more internal strength than I often give myself credit for.

At this stage, I've not yet seen the light at the end of the tunnel, although it seems at times I've seen it as a light coming from an oncoming train. But since I've already been to Hell and back, I can stand on the tracks and let it come at me because I have a lot of inner strength to block it or go through it again.

I've had little emotional support other than from my mother and sisters, so I've tried to restructure my thinking slowly. I may have many blockades, but I still have an undying drive, a fire in me, to keep going on to try new things. I hope that new drugs and other methods of help will be developed.

People suffering with this disorder need to stick together, perhaps lobbying politicians to get more funding for research for better treatment for this disorder. But for people who have difficulty picking up the telephone, such action is difficult. We also have difficulties if we do become part of a group because we feel no one is interested in what we have to say. We are adverse to being ridiculed and feel we've been laughed at enough.

Working with new techniques and making people laugh and smile give my life more meaning, while listening to other people's problems help me grow and get my mind off my mine. From my dot on this planet, I want to somehow spread a little sunshine in this world.

My goals include doing what I can, being a good person, finding some modicum of peace and personal happiness for myself and ultimately sharing it with a special other person. I've been discouraged many times but I have a fond memory of when I lived in Maryland. I wasn't able to tumble in gym class, but a nice woman gave me a little certificate anyway because I tried. That memory has stayed with me and gives me encouragement that there is a reward just in the attempt.

I hope that my story helps and inspires readers. It has come from my gut and I've cried while writing it. But I want others to know there is hope. Maybe writing my story and helping others is a reason why I've gone through all this. Best of luck to all who are reading this book and remember that when people judge you, think twice before listening to them and judging yourself because chances are they have not walked in your shoes.

To all you quiet people, afraid of others and of life, you probably have much good to offer this world. I know that I do and that I deserve to be out there, so I will keep on plugging, chugging, and dancing away with my Panda.

Do -You-Know-You-Are-Berrrrrry-Sta-Wrong?!
by Brenda E. Eads

"Do you know you are very strong?" What could a line from a Sesame Street book about Grover, the monster, have to do with agoraphobia and panic disorder? First of all, I am addressing all of you out there who know first hand about panic and anxiety disorders. You and anyone who cares about you.

In recent times there have been articles, talk shows, and other information about this family of illnesses. That is great and I hope the medical profession is now more aware of this disorder and the many types of treatment. I may not have anything new to say to you, but I want to encourage you to hang in there and not give up. Search, dig, cry, fall, crawl, but get up ... you can do it! Remember, you are very strong. Never forget.

And that brings us back to Grover and his story, "The Monster At the End of This Book." Poor Grover. He is so afraid. There's a monster at the end of his book and he pleads with each reader not to turn the pages and reach that monster! We do turn the pages, however, and each time Grover tries to stop us in various ways. He ties the pages together and nails the pages together and finally builds a strong, thick, brick wall. We readers simply keep turning the pages, going through all his defenses, eventually finding Grover under a pile of broken bricks saying weakly, "Do you know you are very strong?"

The next page is the last page and now Grover is in a state of panic, sweat beading his face. He begs us not to turn it. Of course we do ... and we find after all this time, the terrifying monster was Grover himself ... lovable, fuzzy, and blue. He is so relieved ... and embarrassed at all the fuss he has caused.

It's a terrific book. Check it out of the library. I did. My first acquaintance was made through my niece, April, then three years old. She'd memorized each word perfectly and would "read" to everyone over and over. When she came to the line, "Grover speaks from under the bricks," she would not say it in his puny tones. Instead, April always drew it out proudly and loudly, "DO YOU-KNOW-YOU-ARE-BERRRRRRY-STA-WRONG?!"

I took that funny-faced three year old's words and tucked them inside. Every time the dizzying, terrifying panic symptoms came over me I would take them out and use them as a form of protection. "You can do this," I'd hear whispered to me. "You are very strong." Sometimes I'd hear a gentle chiding, "Don't you remember? You *are* very strong?" And finally these words became a part of me; "I am very strong."

I am strong. I now have passed the nineteen year mark of coping with my own personal panic disorder. It has stolen most of my twenties and all of my thirties. I hate it; hate it so cold and blue-black, I thought nothing could warm it. I'm frightened I will never again be the independent, confident person I once was. That's a major side effect of agoraphobia. It steals you, the essence of the person you always thought you were. Your entire concept of self is altered, leaving you floundering to find an identity.

Like Grover, though, when we first feel the fear and can find no reasonable explanation for it, we begin to do things to help us avoid the awful physical and emotional symptoms that overwhelm us. We tie ourselves to others, often our spouse, parents, or siblings, who make us feel safer. We acquire or construct habits and rituals that limit us, but make us more secure. We may be forced to build more and more defenses to hide behind, but soon, like Grover, we find even that is not enough. The pages of our lives keep turning and we get to the end of our book, only to find the monster that is making us so frightened is us.

Can we overcome this illness when our hating it is the same as hating ourselves? We are intelligent people, rational and responsible. We know it is irrational not to be able to go to the grocery store, teach Sunday School, or even visit our mother. But what we know is not what we feel. Soon the thick, strong walls of our refuge becomes our prison. Who will break down the bricks and tell us, "Do you know you are very strong?"

Maybe only ourselves. Nineteen years of my life have been dominated by anxiety episodes. My daughter has never known me any other way. The symptoms have ebbed and flowed over that period, but in an ever-increasing spiral toward more limitations and phobias.

I've taken two behavior and cognitive courses and spoken with three different psychologists and countless physicians. Some have helped me to deal with the physical and emotional effects of these disorders. Some have done nothing at all.

After participating in their programs, I was not all better, only poorer. I felt even more of a failure because they said X percent got well if they did *this* program and X percent got well if they used *that* program. I was the one out of many who didn't significantly improve, although many others did. Therefore, I figured it must be *my* fault. Maybe I didn't try hard enough or was doing something wrong. I didn't want to believe it was my fault, but they said it was. After all, *they* were the experts.

I began studying the different theories about this illness and they seemed to go around in circles. One group saying, "Anxiety and panic disorder sufferers have a different brain chemistry *because* they are Agoraphobic."

"No!" another faction would state. "Anxiety sufferers have a brain chemistry disorder and *therefore they become* Agora-phobic."

In other words, one says if you choose to think yourself into being crazy, you will become so, and the other one says you're crazy because you can't help your faulty brain chemistry.

Surely by now (?) they realize it is probably a combination of both factors in varying degrees that cause us to be the way we are. I sincerely want to ask them to please forget their opinions and work together to help us. We are dying! If not our physical bodies, our souls and our hopes. Many of us fall into depression, some committing suicide to escape the pain. Some of us have been abandoned by our families and friends. They may think it was our choice to isolate ourselves. How can they know we pushed them away because we couldn't bear to see and feel their concern and love for us any longer, and then also be unable to fix their pain? We can't even fix our own pain.

We're ashamed and embarrassed because this is an un-seen illness, a weakness we think within us. How can something feel so real and not be real? I know a little of each person who I hope is reading this. I know what it is to try and try and have the same feared object or place be just as difficult to face the next time.

At my worst, I was totally house bound for three and a half months. I couldn't even talk on the phone for a brief time. I used to leave notes for the bread delivery man so I wouldn't have to open the door. I read the obituaries faithfully in the daily papers, almost wishing I were reading my own. I didn't want to die. I just didn't want to live if it had to be this way. I was lost and could see no way out. I became so tired of fighting and getting nowhere. One day I just stopped.

Now wait, I didn't say I quit or gave up. I simply stopped and rested. After awhile, I began to sort out what was me and what was other people's expectations of me. It was not an easy task and I have to continue the process frequently. I also stopped hating myself and being ashamed of having panic disorder. It is no different from having cancer or diabetes. It's an illness, no matter what its cause.

I devoured everything I could find on the subject; newsletters, articles, books, and videos. In time I built up an extensive library. I started telling others exactly what my problem was instead of trying to hide it. Some didn't or couldn't understand. Two or three people said I was possessed by an evil spirit or that my house had possessed me (and they thought I was strange.) A few thought I wanted to escape the responsibilities of adulthood, to be taken care of, and to always get my way.

Most did understand, for it is a rare person who reaches adulthood without developing at least one simple phobia. It may be bridges, bats, knives, water, heights, storms, elevators, or anything at all. I used this in my explanations.

For example, ask a bee phobic to visualize going about his or her daily life with an angry bee strolling about on his bare skin or even buzzing around their head. How much could this person accomplish under those circumstances? Listeners quickly get the idea of how difficult it is to live with generalized anxiety or panic episodes. Only we cannot escape from the trigger of our fears as they can because we usually don't know what the trigger is.

There are many therapies to choose from; relaxation therapy, group therapy, meditation, biofeedback, medication, counseling, exercise, cognitive therapy, changing diet, hypnosis, laugh therapy, cry therapy, make-yourself-do-it therapy, and the worst of all; someone-else-trying-to-make-you-do-it therapy.

We all know no one can make an adult do anything if that person doesn't choose to do it, but if you haven't tried all of the above, except for the last one, of course, try some more. If the only way you can get the mail is to walk backwards keeping an eye on your safe place, do it that way. Do whatever you have to do. It may take, as in my case, a combination of therapies and medications, but don't give up. You're worth the effort.

These things I want to leave you. If you are tired ... rest. It is not selfish to take time for yourself. It is very necessary. If you don't feel your present doctor or your treatment is working out for you, find another. It's hard work to recover. Very hard. Follow your intuition or instincts, but always be honest with yourself. You know when you are doing your best.

Last of all, please don't ever stop trying. Tomorrow will be a better day. And if not tomorrow, surely the day after that, I promise. Remember, hold your head high, smile, and say,

"I AM BERRRRRRY STA-WRONG!"

When the window and door seats were taken at the agoraphobics support group meeting, Rachel took matters into her own hands.

Strategies for Coping with Panic

1. Remember that although your feelings and symptoms are very frightening, they are not dangerous or harmful.

2. Understand that what you are experiencing is just an exaggeration of your normal bodily reactions to stress.

3. Do not fight your feelings or try to wish them away. The more you are willing to face them, the less intense they will become.

4. Do not add to your panic by thinking about what "might" happen. If you find yourself asking "What if?" tell yourself "So what!"

5. Stay in the present. Notice what is really happening to you as opposed to what you think might happen.

6. Label your fear level from zero to ten and watch it go up and down. Notice that it does not stay at a very high level for more than a few seconds.

7. When you find yourself thinking about the fear, change your "what if" thinking. Focus on and carry out a simple and manageable task such as counting backwards from 100 by 3's or snapping a rubber band on your wrist.

8. Notice that when you stop adding frightening thoughts to your fear, it begins to fade.

9. When the fear comes, expect and accept it. Wait and give it time to pass without running away from it.

10. Be proud of yourself for your progress thus far, and think about how good you will feel when you succeed this time.

Courtesy Jerilyn Ross, M.A., L.I.C.S.W., The Ross Center for Anxiety and Related Disorders, Inc., Washington DC. Adapted from Mathews et al., 1981.

A Letter to my Sons
by Susan Turner

Dear Jace and Johnny,

Seven and a half years ago, when agoraphobia came crashing into my life, it invaded yours, too. This isn't to say that it didn't affect your dad or the rest of my family, because it did. I really believe now that it's a family disorder.

As I look back on the time when I began my slide into agoraphobia, I can see how you both suffered by what was happening to me. Because you are both individuals with distinct personalities, your reactions and interactions with me were quite different. This letter is my attempt to try to help you understand something that I felt, as a mother, I should shield from you. That I realize now was a gigantic mistake.

I want to share with you my struggle to reclaim my life from a horrific disorder that no one should have to go through. This is not an excuse or justification for any harm that I may have caused you because of my preoccupation with agoraphobia. I did not invite it into our family! It just came unannounced and now I feel it's time to come to terms with how much my disorder affected you both. You know bits and pieces of what was going on, but now allow me to introduce you to the demon, agoraphobia.

The week after Spring break in 1987, I had my first major panic attack. There are three reasons I believe people start having panic attacks; 1) a biochemical imbalance; 2) predisposition; and 3) overwhelming loss. I believe that all these factors came into play that week. We'd just returned from a visit to grandmom and grandpop's house in Vista. As usual, we took the bus because I hadn't driven the freeway in years. Traveling had made me uncomfortable for some time, but I would when I couldn't get out of it. (When I first began having panic attacks, I thought that they just started happening out of the blue. But like the freeway, there were other things I'd been avoiding for years. Since they didn't interfere with my life too much, though, I didn't give any new avoidance much credence.) So you might recall how our visit was a crazy, frantic one, and to top it off, we got stranded at the Glendale bus station when there was no room for us on our bus back to Santa Barbara.

That first week working back at school, I had two major panic attacks. You probably are wondering just what a panic attack is. Well, for me, it's a bunch of physical sensations at the same time. It's feeling faint, hot and cold, having the sensation of the world spinning around me, total fright, feeling like I'm not in control of my body or mind, seeing spots before my eyes, feeling like I'm not really in this world (which is called "depersonalization") and the desperate need to escape wherever I am. I had no idea what was going on with me. Johnny, I don't know if you remember, but you came to the Med Center with me when I was diagnosed. That week changed my life and I know it changed both of yours, too.

Before those attacks, I was always on the run ... never home. I always performed at least 110%. I was the ultimate overachiever. Jace, I know I pushed you, too. You had to be the best student. It was only a year or two ago when we could really begin to be honest with each other. And that's when you told me you felt I loved you conditionally. You believed that if you didn't do well in school, I wouldn't love you. I remember all the years that the three of us would sit at the dining room table and "we" would do your homework! I even went as far as almost doing entire reports for you guys just so you would get an "A." That sure changed the following school year, didn't it?

I want you to know that I began having panic attacks everyday. My life crashed in around me. Jace, that's when I started seeing Don who we both believe is one of the most interesting people we've ever met. He really tried to help. Don put me on some medication, which at that time only calmed me down some, but didn't stop the attacks. I think that's because I was going downhill fast.

The type of therapy we did wasn't working for me, even if I've heard it's helped others. I tried hard to continue on with my life, to keep up the pretense that everything was okay. But I soon avoided everything that once was so important to me. I went to your baseball games if your dad took me, but I spent most of the time clutching the arms of my chair. After one of your games, Johnny, we went to Bob's for dinner, but by the time we got there, I'd made myself sick and we couldn't go in. And Jace, when your last game came, I really wanted to be there to support you. Dad couldn't go, so I decided that I had to try to get there. Unfortunately, your games were at a place more difficult for me to get to. I finally got there but it was about half way through the game because I kept panicking and had to keep turning around. When I did arrive, I couldn't even sit down. I still wanted to be part of the family, but my world was getting smaller and smaller. I could barely drive at that point and dropped out of all my activities except for my job at Peabody School and seeing Don.

Then there was that hot Sunday in May. You guys needed something at La Cumbre Plaza, so I decided to go along for the ride. When we got there, your dad and you two went off. I sat in the car. It didn't take long before it got super hot in the car and I started panicking. I couldn't go into the mall to find you and I couldn't leave. I thought I was going to die! I hadn't started bringing water and my medication everywhere with me yet (but I learned to do that fast.) I got out of the car and walked around it. I got back in the car and crouched down on the floor. When you guys finally returned, I, of course, said nothing. I rode home in silence and I ran into my room when we got home. That was the last time for over a year that we ever went anywhere as a family.

     I never allowed you to see me panic. I'd either get silent or run into my room. I cried my tears in private for what was happening to me and what it was doing to you. Dad started doing all my out in the world activities and would drag one of you along. When you'd ask why I wasn't going instead, my pat answers were "I don't feel well" or "I just can't!" It's hard to really know what I should've said back then because Jace, you were only 12 and Johnny, you were just 10. How could I expect you to understand what your dad and everyone else in our family couldn't? All I do know is that you both were confused and I was sure embarrassed.

I managed finishing out the school year at Peabody, but within weeks I couldn't leave the house. That was that ... homebound! I felt so badly that both of you had to find your own rides to the beach, to friends' houses and everywhere else because I was unable to drive you. Just the year before at this same time, you'd had a different mother, not the "ghost" mother had become. When you would ask me to take you places, again the pat answer was "I can't!" Jace, for most of your life we hadn't gotten along. You knew how to push my buttons and seemed to enjoy seeing me squirm. When you were in the fifth and sixth grades, we actually had a decent relationship, but that changed again when you entered the seventh grade. That summer you stayed away from me as much as you could and when you were around, I felt this tremendous judgment coming from you. I very seldom asked you to help me because it hurt too much to see the disgust and anger (or maybe it was confusion?) in your eyes.

Johnny, you, at that time, just kind of accepted what was going on. Although you did occasionally complain about having to ask other parents to take you places, I didn't see the criticism in your eyes. When you were home we had a good time together. We'd listen to tapes and play games that I allowed you to cheat at! You ran small errands for me without question. I don't know if either of you believe me, but I really did try my best to not have my disorder (which had developed into agoraphobia) interfere with your lives too much.

I know I wasn't there for you emotionally. I was barely surviving and there really wasn't much room left in my thoughts for you both. Johnny, I remember you getting so irate with me when I'd ask you a question. You'd answer me and a few minutes later I'd ask you the same question again because in the space of time it took for you to answer me, I was already consumed with my latest symptom. I can't believe how self-absorbed I became. It's hard to even imagine what it was like for you to see your once active, "normal" mother laying on the couch or in her bedroom most of the summer like some kind of invalid. For a few years, except when your dad wasn't working out of town, you basically raised yourselves.

In September, when I began seeing Kathy and making progress, I want you to know I was doing the hard and scary work, not only for myself, but for you, too. I wanted to be a mother again; a mother you would not have to make excuses for and be ashamed of.

As my recovery progressed and I began driving again, I want to thank you, Johnny, for being my companion. Even though you couldn't drive, I felt safer with you in the car. Jace, I hope you realize this isn't a "Jace bashing letter" because we already have discussed much of what I'm writing about. We've made our peace and I truly believe we now are good friends, confidants, and have the best mother/son relationship we've ever had. But back then you weren't there for me. I blamed you for awhile because, after all, you were the oldest! Although I didn't ask you if you would come on walks and drives with me, I suppose I'd just hoped you'd offer. When you didn't, I'd be mad at you in silence. Writing this letter to you and your brother has opened my eyes to some ugliness that I never really considered before. Johnny, again at that time, was easy to love and gave his love unconditionally. Johnny was an uncomplicated child. You, on the other hand, weren't. You were closed off and not easy to show love and affection to. Interestingly enough, you were then and still are too much like me! I wanted your approval and love so desperately that I now believe that as you turned away from me, I in turn, turned away from you. I never felt I measured up as a mother anyway and then when I began dealing with agoraphobia, I knew I wasn't being the mother I always wanted to be for you. So to steel myself from your disapproving glares, I didn't allow or invite you to become part of my recovery process.

It's 1994 as I write this and we have all survived the worst part of my dealing with agoraphobia somewhat intact, although I still have work to do. About a month ago, Johnny, as we were driving somewhere, you commented that just a few years ago I was unable to do that. It's statements like those that are a fantastic reminder of how far I have come. Times like these when I'm doing what other mothers can do are the payoffs for all frightening hard work I've done. Many parents get mad when they have to chauffeur their kids around.

They take it for granted they can do it. I have done this for awhile now myself. But just last week when you asked me to take you to a friend's house, I remembered that there was a time only a few years ago when I would have said, "I can't!" I was filled with a wonderful warm glow.

Jace, before your short-lived move to Seattle last March, we had a heart to heart about how my agoraphobia affected you. You were honest enough to say that, yes, you had been angry with me during the time when I was severely limited, but as you grew older, you realized how courageous I really was in my battle against the demon, agoraphobia. That meant a lot to me. Although we've been building a relationship now for over a year and a half, I think your feelings about that time in all our lives has stood between us. You are both grown up now; Jace, you are almost 21, and Johnny, my baby, you are 18. Even though you are not children anymore and some might say, "Let the past stay in the past," I can't. Not yet.

I have a lot of guilt for all I couldn't do for you and all the moments I missed sharing with you when I was a homebound agoraphobic. It's important for my healing and recovery as well as yours that I apologize to you. I didn't ask to have agoraphobia and you didn't ask for a mother who for a time was only "physically" there for you, a person who for all intents and purposes, was only taking up space.

Jace, first and foremost, I want to apologize for honoring the boundaries that I felt you didn't want me to break through, but in reality, you were screaming out for me to smash down. Because I didn't, you turned to women like Sheryl and Vicki to be your surrogate mothers. They gave you what I wasn't able to at that time. I'm sorry for not being able to give you the physical love you desperately yearned for, but I didn't even know you needed it. I'm sorry for missing your high school graduation, school events, the chance to see you row, and all but one of your basketball games.

Johnny, I cannot express to you how sorry I am for not being able to come to the hospital when you fell down that 50 foot cliff. I don't know if you asked for me. If you did, your dad was compassionate enough to not tell me. Of all the things I avoided because of my agoraphobia, this is one that will haunt me forever. I apologize for not attending your eighth grade graduation, all school functions, Boy Scout ceremonies, your last two years playing baseball, and for all the hundreds of times you had to ask other parents to take you places.

To both of you, I'm sure there are many things that I have forgotten, so I am apologizing for those things, too. I am so sorry for all the embarrassment and shame I know I have caused you by having to explain to your friends what the hell was going on with me, for not allowing you to have friends spend the night because I was uncomfortable with anyone other than family in the house, and especially for you having to attend my only brother's wedding and my loving daddy's funeral without me. Were you wondering what people were saying about me? I am truly sorry for the time that you lived with a mother who was perpetually anxious, depressed, distracted, and in another ozone... a mother who couldn't concentrate long enough to help you with your homework. (Johnny, I bet you liked that, though!) During the last eight years, you have both gone through your own stuff and although I feel my dealings with agoraphobia didn't cause them, they may have contributed to it and again, for that, I am sorry.

Jace, during the last year, we have done some forgiving and healing work, but there still is more to be done. Johnny, knowing you, you probably feel that what happened in the past is over, but it isn't. I hope one day you both can really forgive me, if not for me, then for yourselves. I am learning to give myself some slack and I am beginning to forgive myself, also.

I loved you then, I love you now, and I will love you both unconditionally until I die.

Dear Mom
by Johnny Turner

Dear Mom,

I am writing in response to your letter to Jace and me. You were very concerned about how we fared during what you termed, your eight and a half years battling the demon ... agoraphobia.

When the Demon came into our family, I was almost ten years old. I was too young to really realize what was going on. You tried very hard to explain what agoraphobia was. But even after many explanations, I still didn't understand. So I just came to accept the way you had changed. I know you did nothing intentionally to hurt my life. You may not have been there for everything I needed ... but that's life!

I was very young when Dad told me something that has stuck with me to this day. He said that life wasn't always fair and people just have to live with whatever comes their way. So I learned to live with a "different" mother.

What I think wasn't fair during the time when you couldn't leave the house wasn't that Jace and I didn't have a "normal" mother who could take us places, go to school functions, etc. It was that you had your life stolen away from you. You were afraid of everything and you couldn't live the life you once had.

You don't have to apologize for not being "there" for me emotionally or physically. I don't feel I was harmed by that. I think in many ways you did me a favor. I learned to take care of my own emotional needs. I also had to learn to solve most of my own problems. I guess, in a way, the demon helped me grow up and become more independent. Some people may say that 10, 11, and even 12 is too early for a kid to learn independence. I don't agree, at least in my case. I never blamed or disliked you for how all our lives changed. I knew it wasn't your fault. And I knew that no matter what you were going through, you loved me. Hell, if you didn't, you would have kicked me out a long time ago.

I hope you don't blame yourself for the way I

turned out. How I have chosen to live my life has nothing to do with the few years you felt you neglected me. Believe me, it has nothing to do with your demon. As you well know, I have always thought the way I wanted to think and have done whatever I thought I could get away with. I have done some things in my life that you would not have approved of, but I was doing some of them before your dealings with agoraphobia. Even if you never had agoraphobia, I still would have been up to "no good."

Please don't even ask for my forgiveness. There is nothing to forgive. You never back stabbed me, hurt me, or did anything wrong. You were just trying to survive and beat that demon that you pretty much have. If anyone should ask for forgiveness, it should be Jace and me for not helping out our own mom more than we did.

I think it is important that I answer some of the things you mentioned in your letter that you felt affected me and made such a negative impact on my life. The things that really didn't matter much to me were helping me with my homework and going to my eighth grade graduation. As you well know, I never wanted to do my homework, anyway. So you not being on me about it allowed me to do as little as I could get away with. Sorry! As for my eighth grade graduation, I didn't want to go through the ceremony. I thought it was stupid. You were the one who told me that someday I might regret not going on stage to get my diploma. So I went through the ceremony without a thought of you not being there.

Some things were kind of hard for me, though, like trying to tell my friends why you weren't working at school, coming to my games, or picking me up anymore. They would say, "Where is your mom?" or "Why can't your mom pick you up?" I would tell them that you had a problem, but they wouldn't accept that answer. They kept at me until I would get really mad. After awhile, even they stopped asking. I guess when I first woke up in the hospital after falling down that cliff and didn't see you next to me, I was sad. Dad was there, though, and Jace came to visit me. When I came home from the hospital you took good care of me. As for not coming to my baseball games or seeing me receive my badges at the Boy Scout ceremonies, I felt a different kind of sadness. You were always there when I got into trouble. You were the one who had to talk to my teachers when they called. And you were the one who, unhappily, signed my not great report cards. I wish you could have seen me receiving awards at Boy Scouts or getting on base or catching a ball at my games. It just seemed to me that you were there for the bad things but not for the good things for awhile.

The one thing that made me kind of mad, was not being allowed to have friends come over our house for a year or two. I couldn't understand it. All my friends could have friends over and I once could, but no more. As for not taking me places or picking me up, I liked that. It gave me extra time to do what I wanted to do.

When I read in your letter how much it meant to you that we played games and listened to tapes together, that surprised me. I was just having fun doing those things with you. I remember when you started driving again. Every night I would go with you (even though I couldn't drive, you said you felt better with me sitting next to you) in the car and we would drive down to the Mobil station to buy candy. I was so proud of you for trying to drive.

Mom, I want to tell you again that I was not embarrassed or disappointed in you when you were severely agoraphobic. I admire you for having the courage to fight as hard as you did to win back your life. I'm also proud of you for dedicating your life to helping others who suffer with agoraphobia. In fact, by seeing you deal with this disorder, you opened my eyes and helped me to be more understanding of people who have emotional problems. I just hope that all the others out in the world with agoraphobia can beat their demons, too.

Mom, try not to feel too badly about Jace and me. We should be the ones who are sorry because you weren't able to enjoy those years like we could. We were able to leave our house and have a life.

Your beloved son,

Johnny

My Mother's Statue
by Jace Ryan Turner

At the age of twelve
i was left
before the altar
i had created,
alone.
The absence of this
shrine
whose blood gave
life
to mine
kneeled vacant
in her shaking body,
staring at the statue
she had once created;
a statue pinned to life
now trembled by fear,
was masked in disbelief
by her eyes
anger in mine.
    *

I'd remember back
at the times
we'd spend at the beach
with her friends
and mine
and the smiles
so many smiles.
And when embodied
by the ocean's liquid blue
i'd sneak a glimpse
of her

pouring in pride.
How magnificent she
seemed
bronzed by the golden sun,
teeth peering like
tiny stars,
the one's you make
wishes from.
                    *

Then i'd wake
from those currents of
memories,
the kind you'd like
to live in,
and see my
Mother's body,
a still life,
imprisoned in the painting
of her house,
engrossed by everything
in her new existence
but me.
And where was i?
still in the garden of youth
growing tensions
in the bottom of a well,
my heart,
drowning in resentment
for the, now
pale hand
that ceased to caress
my emotional needs;
despising the lifeless figure that
withdrew all the freedom
from my body
except the walking
of my two legs.
And there i stood

wallowing in my anger,
as intense as the sun
at noon, in the midst
of a most unbearable
summer heat.
Blinded
to my shrine
who'd at one time
cast a shadow over
my body from
such heat,
retreated into her own
10x10 world of
walls and safety
and let me
blister.
*

At the age of twenty-one
my mind is clearer now.
Through the growth of
nine giant steps
for both
myself and my mother
we've again
come together.
Though not to say,
it was easy
because there were
many setbacks.
But each time
a tiny wound was healed,
an exquisite flower
grew
in place
mending the soil
to which was
robbed.
*

When several chapters of the phobia group had a field trip to the grocery store, a unique traffic pattern was created.

What to Do if a Family Member Has an Anxiety Disorder

1. Don't make assumptions about what the affected person needs; ask them.

2. Be predictable; don't surprise them.

3. Let the person with the disorder set the pace for recovery.

4. Find something positive in every experience. If the affected person is only able to go part way to a particular goal, such as a movie theater or party, consider that an achievement rather than a failure.

5. Don't enable avoidance: negotiate with the person with panic disorder to take one step forward when he or she wants to avoid something.

6. Don't sacrifice your own life and build resentments.

7. Don't panic when the person with the disorder panics.

8. Remember that it's all right to be anxious yourself; it's natural for you to be

concerned and even worried about the person with panic disorder.

9. Be patient and accepting, but don't settle for the affected person being permanently disabled.

10. Say: "You can do it no matter how you feel. I am proud of you. Tell me what you need now. Breathe slow and low. Stay in the present. It's not the place that's bothering you, it's the thought. I know that what you are feeling is painful, but it's not dangerous. You are courageous."

Don't say: "Relax. Calm down. Don't be anxious. Let's see if you can do this (i.e., setting up a test for the affected person). You can fight this. What should we do next? Don't be ridiculous. You *have* to stay. Don't be a coward."

Adapted from Sally Winston, Psy. D., The Anxiety and Stress Disorders Institute of Maryland, Towson, MD, 1992.

She Just Wouldn't Go
by Brenda E. Eads

"Tory, I'm home," Jeff's deep voice boomed throughout the neatly kept house. He waited. There was no reply. Taking the stairs two at a time, he looked in the bedroom and the bathroom. "Honey, where are you?" No Tory. No bouncing black poodle skittering around his ankles in greeting either.

A faint feeling of unease fluttered in his stomach, but only someone who knew him well would have noticed the tightening of the skin across his prominent cheekbones.

Jeff crossed the back porch, vaguely aware of Tory's flowers, heavy with buds. For weeks she had been waiting for this new miniature rose to bloom. His brown eyes sharply scanned the yard, then the pond and the pasture. There was no indication of movement. No small figure, dark hair tucked behind her ears. No spot of black at her heels.

"Tory! Where are you?" he shouted. She was always there when he came home. She wouldn't just go. She couldn't.

Returning inside, he searched briefly for a note or some sign. There was nothing. Jeff suddenly noticed how empty the house felt without her.

He walked up, then down the gravel road in front of their house. He returned just in time to hear the phone ring, grabbing it with a surge of hope. It was Tory's mother, Betty.

"Hi Jeff, can I talk to Tory?"

"Uh, no. She's outside right now. I'll have her call you when she comes in, okay?"

"That will be fine. I just need her to water my flowers while we're away this week. How's her roses coming along?"

Jeff cleared his throat, "They're fine."

"Is everything all right, Jeff?" You sound funny."

"Everything is fine. I'll have her call you."

Tory's mother didn't sound convinced. Betty was sharp, almost as intuitive as Tory. He swore they both read minds. Tory got her love for flowers from Betty, too. Certain they sensed she cared about them when she talked to them. And that dog, that ridiculous scrap of jet black curls she called Boby. They communicated without speaking at all.

Jeff pushed a tanned hand through his blonde hair. The thought repeated. Where are you, Tory?

Icy fingers of panic crawled up and down Tory's back, aware she was not in the right place. These walls were yellow, not soft rose and cream. Instead of lacy ruffled priscillas, bright patterned blinds covered the windows.

The only thing familiar to her was the warmth curled behind her knees. Tory reached out and tentatively caressed the soft head. "Boby," she whispered. "Where are we?"

Sliding off the bed and cradling the small dog tightly to her chest, the acid taste of fear burned in her throat. There were no sounds. "You're all right. Calm down. You're all right." she repeated over and over under her breath.

Breathing deeply from the stomach, as she had been taught, she walked to the door and tried the knob. It turned easily at her touch. Tory entered another brightly painted room. She had never seen this place before.

"Barry," Jeff said with relief, "I'm so glad you could come."

"Of course. You sounded awful worried on the phone."

I can't find Tory anywhere. She's gone."

"Gone?"

Jeff paced. I can't find Boby either."

Barry studied his friend's worried face. "Have you checked with anyone, her parents or friends? From what you've told me, she wouldn't go away by herself."

Jeff sighed. "Her mother called. She doesn't know anything. I didn't tell her Tory wasn't here."

"Why not?" Barry asked.

Jeff hesitated. "Barry, aside from her doctor, you're the only one who knows the whole story. Even her parents don't know how much her problem has affected her."

Why? You ashamed of her?"

"Of course not! "I love her! Tory's the best thing that ever happened to me, even with her disability."

Barry placed a calming hand on his friend's shoulder. "You've got to face it old buddy. It's a mental illness."

Jeff felt impatient. "It isn't. Not in the way you mean. You see now why we don't tell many people? You don't even understand and I've told you all about it. We don't want or need people's misunderstanding or pity. We just need their acceptance, the same as if she had diabetes or cancer!"

"All right, calm down. Now is not the time to argue about it. What are you going to do? Call the police?"

"I don't know," Jeff said heavily. "They wouldn't take me seriously if I reported my wife missing after only two hours." He kneaded his lean belly and ruefully said, "Tory has tried to tell me how her stomach feels when she's afraid. I can identify with every word she said now."

"Maybe you could call her doctor," Barry suggested.

Jeff's face showed relief. "Dr. Ross. I didn't think of that. I'll look up her number."

Jeff dug through the papers Tory had stacked in a basket by her favorite chair. Sheepishly he looked at Barry. "Tory always takes care of the paperwork around here."

"Got it," he said five minutes later.

"Jessica Ross," the crisp voice answered.

"Dr. Ross, this is Jeffrey Edmonds. I'm sorry to bother you at home."

"Yes Jeff, what can I do for you?"

"It's Tory. She's nowhere around!"

What do you mean?"

"I don't know. I came home and she's just not here."

"I recommend calling the authorities. You know Tory would not go anywhere without you at this stage."

"I know Dr. Ross, but will you help me explain her condition. They won't understand."

"Call them Jeff. I'll be there in thirty minutes."

Dr. Ross arrived first. Jeff wiped his damp hand down his thigh before shaking hers. He'd never been at ease with her, but Tory liked and trusted her. In the year since seeing Dr. Ross, she'd gotten healthier. The other doctor Tory had seen hadn't helped at all, never seeming to understand how frightened she was much of the time, unless at home. Maybe worse of all, Tory felt uncomfortable with his manner, and how he treated her illness.

The county deputy came and Jeff was relieved to see it was Tom Jenkins, an acquaintance of his.

Tom was puzzled. "I've heard of recluses who never see anyone or leave their homes, but Jeff, Tory seems as normal as you and me. You'll have to explain more."

Jeff started, "Well, Tory has this phobia. "Well, we all fear something, like heights or some kind of animal..."

Tom broke in, "Yeah, for me it's caves. They give me the shivers."

"Yes, like that, only with Tory, she's not afraid of anything specific. I guess she's mostly afraid of herself; how she'll react in situations. That she'll get sick or not able to ... "

Dr. Ross cut in smoothly as Jeff looked helplessly at her. "Tory has a condition called agoraphobia. She functions quite normally in most situations as long as she's in a place she considers safe, such as home, or if she is with a safe person. In Tory's case this is Jeff."

"Is she a threat to herself or anyone else, Doc?"

"Oh, no, Tory is completely rational. She knows it's unreasonable to panic when there is nothing to be afraid of, but she can't control it."

"Well, what causes this?"

"Some experts think it is a chemical imbalance of the brain, the part that controls our "Fight or Flight" reflex. Others believe it's caused by a trauma."

Tom wrote this all down in his notebook. "Well, tell me this. If we found Tory, how would she react to us?"

Dr. Ross considered his words carefully. "Tory's anxiety is going to be high. My advice is to take your cues from her. Let her be in control as much as possible. Don't swoop down on her and take her choices away if you can help it. That's what Tory fears most of all; loss of control."

"I see. Well, Jeff, Dr. Ross, I'll do what I can. Is there anything else I should know?"

"Yeah. Her dog is gone, too."

"Dog, what kind of dog? Any protection to her?"

Jeff almost smiled. "Boby is a black toy poodle, about eight pounds. He's never even growled at anyone, let alone bite. Hey ... wait a minute, Boby is on medication for a heart murmur. She never misses giving him his pills."

"Check if the dog's medication is still here," Tom said.

Barry returned from the kitchen, pills in hand.

"Tory's crazy about that dog," Jeff said. "She would never leave his pills if she had a choice."

"This is what I want you to do, the deputy said. Call family, friends, anyone you can think of. Find out the last time anyone saw her or talked to her. I'll be in touch."

"I've got to get back to the pharmacy, Barry said. Call me later if you need me."

Dr. Ross rose to leave, too. She tried to comfort Jeff. "You know Tory is recovering, don't you?"

"Yes," Jeff agreed. "

"I want you to know that wherever Tory is, she has the skills to cope as well or even better than a non-phobic person, if she keeps her head. I've seen a great change in her in the last few months."

Jeff's voice caught and he could hardly speak the words. "But what if this person hurts her?"

"Try not to think negatively. Tory is very strong. Think about these last years she's been dealing with this phobic condition. She has never allowed it to kill her hope that tomorrow will be a better day."

"Yes, you're right," Jeff said. "Tory is stronger than I am in some ways, but so helpless in others."

"Just as we all are," said Dr. Ross.

Tory's one thought was to find a phone and call Jeff. He was her lifeline. This need overrode all others at this time. She edged around the rooms searching for the instrument that would free her from this nightmare, but there was none. "Okay, no phone," she said to herself. "Now what?"

"All right, deal with what you have to now." She thought of Dr. Ross and what they had talked about in their sessions. "Just take it one step at a time, Tory. No what ifs."

She looked again through the three rooms. One door was locked from the outside. From the windows, she saw she was on the second floor. Another house was in the distance, but it seemed to be in a sparsely populated rural area.

There is no threat to me right at this moment, she thought. I'm as calm as I can manage under the circumstances. What is the first step? To get out. Tory's mind leapt from getting out to begging for a ride from a passerby. She pictured being confined in a car with a stranger. Whoa! Panic threatened to overwhelm her once more.

Pacing, she fought to control the adrenaline racing over her body. Her stomach churned, feeling she'd vomit or need to use the bathroom immediately. Flopping into a rocking chair she commanded herself. "Breathe. Panic is only fear without oxygen." That's what Dr. Ross always said.

Boby begged with his eyes to sit on Tory's lap. She gave a small signal and he settled there. Closing her eyes, Tory relaxed her tense muscles one by one. She prayed and looked deep in her mind. She felt fear and anxiety, but this was a scary situation. Even a non-phobic would feel fear.

Tory turned her thoughts toward home; the peace she felt when she was out in the yard with her flowers. The sunshine glinting on the pond. Concentrating harder on the picture, Tory could almost smell the warm moist earth and see one brilliant blade of green grass with a tiny ladybug carefully climbing up the underside of it. A soft spring wind caressed her cheek and she was there at peace.

All this time, Tory continued to pet Boby's head and rhythmically rocked in the chair. Suddenly aware of her dry mouth, Tory searched for a sip of water. The thought of food sickened her, but she realized Boby might be hungry. She found some milk and bread in the tiny kitchen and put it before Boby in a bowl.

"I know you're not suppose to have people food but this time it's all we've got."

Satisfied, Boby bent back to the bowl and began to eat. When the last drop was gone and the bowl was licked clean, he looked at Tory as if to say, "Okay, that's done. Now what are we going to do?"

Tory rested on the floor. She spoke to the attentive dog, "The next step is to figure out why and how we got here. Then I promise I'll get us home." She thought she was promising Boby but in reality she was promising herself.

Jeff awoke the next morning with a feeling of dread. He groaned when he recalled talking to Tory's parents. It had been difficult to watch her mother, quietly seeming to search inwardly for some sense her only daughter was all right.

Jeff took the day off. How could he possibly work or concentrate? His whole world seemed upside down.

Weary, he got out of bed and started making breakfast. The toot of a horn made Jeff abandon his meager breakfast and see who was there. It was the mailman.

Jeff was puzzled. "Do you have something too big for the box?"

The friendly looking man said, "Nope. I was just letting Tory know the mail was here.

"Do you honk every day?"

"Yep. Tory always has a wave or a smile for me, and sometimes some of those famous chocolate chip cookies of hers."

"Tell me, did you talk to Tory yesterday?"

The mailman noticed the strain in his face and became serious. "Yep, 'bout ten o'clock. Tory had just made some corn muffins and brought me out one. She couldn't chat. Said someone had dropped by and she was talking to them."

"Did she act any differently than usual?"

"She acted fine. Say, what's goin' on here?"

"Tory's missing, Jeff blurted. "She just disappeared."

Worry and sadness made several sets of creases in the mailman's weathered face. "How can I help?" he asked.

"I don't know," Jeff said. "If anyone else on your route is home, could you ask them if they've seen Tory or Boby?"

"The little dog is gone, too?"

"Yes."

"Well, I hope he's with her. That critter was so attached to Tory he'd pine away if he was apart from her."

Jeff managed to thank him, but on the way back to the house he thought he might pine away, too.

During the day, the phone rang off the hook. He was amazed at the people who knew Tory. Many he didn't know himself. Because of her phobias, she didn't socialize outside their home unless together. Jeff didn't know that Tory had friends that called regularly and stopped by.

The day ended with Jeff no closer to knowing where Tory was than when he had gotten up that morning. He looked one last time out the back door, straining as far as he could see. There was nothing.

The bud on one of Tory's prize roses was just opening. Jeff felt like hurling it out the door. They would only be beautiful if Tory were there to see them. He went to bed, only to toss and turn wearily until he fell into an uneasy sleep.

Tory's day was quite different. No visitors disturbed her. Stiff and sore she awoke on the kitchen floor. She faced the facts. She was in two prisons; one of someone else's making and one of her own. Even if the door were unlocked, she would still be in the prison of her fears.

An unfamiliar feeling swept over Tory. It was anger, something she'd suppressed all her life. It was easier to say it didn't matter than to feel anger. But now she was aware that anger was energy and strength. How dare this person invade her life, taking her from home against her will? They had no right to do that. She'd never butted into anyone else's life. Why did someone feel they had the right to infringe on hers?

Spying a familiar bottle on the stand, all the anger drained away as she reached for it with a trembling hand. It was Boby's pills. Had they been there all the time? She carefully looked over this place she was confined in.

There were books by her favorite author and needlework materials. The kitchen had plenty of canned and frozen food. All she'd need for a week or more was provided.

Tory relaxed. She knew whoever had brought her here was not going to harm her. Her anger returned.

Tory began to plan. She would wait until dark. She was more comfortable in the dark. No one could see her if she freaked out. She never had, but there was always a first time.

Coolly determined, she felt the first pangs of hunger since she had found herself there. Heating some soup, she shared it with Boby. It almost tasted good.

Settling in the rocking chair, she tried to rest. She'd need all her strength, both physical and emotional, to do what she had to do tonight.

After midnight, Tory awakened from her light doze, her mind awhirl. What first? It was only a two story building. If she hung from the window sill, it wouldn't be that far of a drop. She decided which window to use, but many layers of paint had sealed it shut. Casting aside a dearly held value, respect for other people's property, the lamp made a satisfying crash as she flung it through the glass.

After picking out the jagged edges, she peered out.

Tory pulled on an oversized hooded sweatshirt she found in the closet and tucked it into her jeans. "Don't be afraid." Then Tory stuck the trusting poodle in the shirt. When he was securely resting against her side, she threw her other supplies out the window and climbed onto the sill.

With an surge of excitement, accomplishment, and fear, she shouted in her mind. "Jeff, I'm on my way home!"

Seconds later, hanging from the broken frame, she almost wanted to climb back in again. In a strange way, she was leaving a safe place. There she had everything she needed except freedom, but freedom meant more than anything else now. More important than safety. More important than fear. This gave her the courage to let go.

After hitting the ground, Tory pulled Boby from his nest. "One prison down, one to go." Tory took a deep breath, squared her shoulders, and marched down the dark road.

Jeff awoke from a frightening dream. He'd been helpless and afraid, feelings he'd seldom felt before. He needed someone to rescue him. The last of the dream echoed in his ears in Tory's voice. "Jeff, I'm on my way home."

"Keep close, Boby. I'm not sure yet where we are. If you get tired, I'll carry you. I know your legs are short, okay? I'll find a road sign soon, then maybe I'll know where we are."

Tory fell silent then, but her thoughts continued. If I were normal, I could go to a house and get help. Can I do that? Maybe. Could I stop a car? No. That would be foolish, even for a normal person. Don't beat yourself up over that.

What was scarier? Walking miles down a dark road or approaching someone for help? It was a toss up at the moment. She scooped Boby up. "You want to ride awhile? You're cold, too. It's a chilly night." Tory tucked Boby into her sweatshirt and zipped it up so just his head stuck out.

Jeff slept again as Tory walked alone in the night. His dreams returned and he was back in high school. Confused, he tried to find his next class, but his schedule was missing He was relieved at last to see the wrinkle square of yellow paper that told him what to do. As he read it, his hopes were dashed. It only said in smudged writing, "Ask Tory."

He got up and walked through the silent house. He saw reminders of his wife everywhere. The neat list of his appointments in her handwriting, along side of this month's bills ready to mail. His favorite dessert tempting him in the kitchen. His clothes for the next day hanging in a complete outfit because he hated to choose his own clothes.

The realization of what "Ask Tory" meant dawned on him. Maybe Tory needed him less than he needed her.

Jeff saw now the small ways she'd tried to make him more independent. She'd encourage him to take an interest in balancing the checkbook, saying there was a problem she couldn't figure out. She could have. Once in awhile, he would have to cook a simple meal or put the laundry in the dryer if Tory was busy outside. He hated making phones calls, but lately she had other legitimate tasks to do and had told him gently that he had a mouth. He could use it.

"Probably Dr. Ross's suggestions," he muttered, but he knew it was right for him to do these things.

Car lights appeared in the distance and like a deer scenting danger, Tory scurried into the brush on the berm and crouched there, her chest heaving. It was important to be invisible. She felt she could handle panic if she were alone.

After what seemed like hours of walking, Tory came to a section of road hemmed in with trees. She walked into the blackness, as if she were blind. She couldn't even see her feet.

Racing along, the wind roaring past her face. The bumps of the gravel road grasped at her feet as she walked. Boby's claws dug into her ribs as she stumbled up a small rise right into the path of what appeared to be an enormous truck.

Breaks squealed. In the glare of the headlights, Tory partially skidded underneath the vehicle and her sneakered foot wedged up against the front tire.

Dazed, she laid there as the door was flung open and a shadowy figure stood over her. At that moment, Tory gave up. She'd hung from a second story window, walked miles down a pitch black road, all the while fighting the hardest battle with her phobic self ... and she was tired.

Tory heard a muffled yap and realized Boby was still in her jacket. Gentle hands reached out and released the little dog. A familiar voice said, "Tory girl, is that you?"

Near dawn, Jeff was awakened again, this time by pounding on the door. He was surprised to see it was Barry. "What are you doing up so early?"

Barry was pale. "Have you heard from Tory yet?"

Jeff shook his head no.

Barry blurted out, "She's gone."

Jeff didn't understand. "What are you talking about?"

"Jeff, I'm sorry." Barry licked his lips nervously, then went on. "I don't know why I let that doctor talk me into it."

"Tory, answer me! Are you all right?"

Tory slowly focused her eyes and looked into the worried face of her friend, the mailman. The monstrous vehicle became the battered pickup she saw every day. Relief flowed through her and her legs felt as rubbery as Jell-O.

"Is Boby okay?" she whispered.

"He's fine now. Let's see about you."

Helping Tory to her feet, they found she was all right except for scratches and a twisted ankle where it hit the tire.

Tory was confused at how he had come to be there. "What are you doing here in the middle of the night?"

"It's not the middle of the night, girl, it's almost dawn and I'm on my way to pick up the mail for my morning route. The question is, what are you doing here?"

"It's a long story," Tory said. "I'm not even sure."

"Well, no matter. Let's get you home." He looked at her with wise old eyes.

Tory stared intently at him. She was only a few miles from home now. She could hobble there if she chose to. The decision was made. She could trust him and more she could trust herself. After all, what was five minutes in a truck with a friend compared to all that she'd been through?

Barry circled Jeff warily, not sure how his friend would react. Jeff was normally a mild-tempered man, but he was very large and strong. Barry had no doubt he was in serious trouble.

"It was Dr. Nerone. He told me you were bad for Tory, that she needed out from under your influence. He convinced me I was doing the right thing..." his voice trailed off.

"That quack! How did you meet up with him?"

He called about a prescription one day and we got on the subject and before you knew it, he had me halfway convinced. A few more calls, and guess he talked me into it. You know, doctor's authority and all that stuff."

"Why do you think Tory stopped seeing him?! He was making her worse!"

"I didn't think. I just reacted to what he said."

"How did you get her away from home?"

Barry swallowed hard, "Well, Dr. Nerone prescribed this mild sedative and I put it in her coffee that morning ..."

Jeff remembered what the mailman had said, pictured Tory having coffee and muffins with Barry, never expecting a friend to betray her trust that way. "All right, that's enough." Jeff stepped close enough that Barry could feel the puff of his breath as he spoke soft, but stern. "Where is my wife?"

"I don't know." Barry explained how he'd taken Tory to a house he was renovating for a rental. "The first night I went back after I left your house. I took Boby's pills and left them for her while she slept. Later, I had second thoughts. I'm sorry, I tried to fix it, but she wasn't there anymore."

Barry fell silent watching anxiously for Jeff's reaction. He saw his friend's eyes go from rage to great sadness.

Jeff choked out, "Barry, you are my best friend. How could you do this? Tory means so much to me."

In a moment of clarity, Barry said, "Yes, I know, and now I think you do, too."

They heard the toot of a horn. "That's just the mailman," Jeff said, "I talked to him yesterday. Maybe he has some news for me."

The mailman's face creased in a grin as he came around the truck and opened the passenger door. "Gotta Special Delivery for you."

Tears of relief and happiness were on Tory's cheeks. Smudging them away with a grimy hand, she noticed Barry standing behind Jeff.

"It was you!" she spat out. "You come to my house and ... How could you come into my home as a friend and do that to me?" She clenched her hands into fists to help her control herself. "You had no right."

Jeff tried to calm Tory. "It's all right," he said.

Tory had had enough. "It's not all right." At Jeff's shocked look she went on. "Barry treated me like a rag doll, lifting me up from here and putting me down there, like I had no say."

Her voice rose, "You do almost the same thing, only out of kindness and love! On one hand you keep every bump and hard place out of my way, like I'm a child, like you know everything that is best for me. On the other hand, you expect me to take care of everything around here, while you do your thing." The sweep of her arm encompassed the whole farm.

She drew a deep sobbing breath. "I got so confused, I didn't know what I was supposed to be, responsible or helpless."

A touch of sarcasm crept into her voice. "Everybody is always doing what's best for little Tory. For my own good. Well, nobody ever remembered to ask my opinion!"

She smiled bitterly at their stunned expressions. She turned on her heel and limped smartly toward the house throwing one last shot over her shoulder. "Tory left this house two days ago, not of her own free will, but Tory did not come back. A for real grown up, adult woman, Victoria did! Because she chose to."

Jeff ducked as Tory, still on her tirade, flung clothing out of the bathroom door. She slammed the door and he heard the swish of water as she stepped into the tub.

It seemed like hours later the sounds of the drain gurgling came to his ears. Jeff hesitated outside the door. He was afraid. They had been married over seven years, but who was this person? Not the Tory he knew.

He knocked. "Can I come in?"

The lock clicked. He took that for a "yes." Tory was rubbing a newly clean Boby dry. Dressed in a short terry cloth wrap, Jeff easily surveyed the damages of her nights out. There were scratches and skinned up patches on her legs, a nasty - looking bruise on her cheek where the stone had hit her, and cuts across the palms of both hands.

He felt a surge of love and compassion. "If you say, my poor Tory, I'll slap your ears right off your head!"

"We need to talk before I lose my courage."

"Yes we do," agreed Jeff. "And I'll start."

Tory was surprised. "All right, go ahead."

"When you were gone, I realized how much you do around here. I thought I was the big cheese and everything depended on me because of your phobias. I was wrong. I might be an important cog, but you, my love, are the grease. Without you everything came to a screeching halt."

"I know that," Tory said. "But for a long time it didn't matter. Then when it did, you were spoiled and didn't want things to change."

Jeff winced as she said "spoiled," but he knew it was true. Tory went on. "I've been "Miss Do It" ever since I was a little girl. Anything anyone asked me to do, I did, and convinced myself I wanted to, even if I didn't. I did it because I wanted approval. I wanted others to like me. But maybe part of my agoraphobia is a subconscious way for me to make you responsible for some of my needs because I've felt overwhelmed by yours. I can't be the same as I was. I can't do it anymore. We need a balance."

"What do you want me to do?" Jeff asked.

"I just want both of us to be fully independent, able to go it alone if we ever have to." Tory said.

Jeff felt lost. If Tory doesn't need me, he thought, why would she stay with me?"

Sensing his thoughts, Tory put her battered hand on his cheek. "I'll always want you because I love you very much. No matter what our problems, I wouldn't trade you for any other man I know. You are a rare thing Jeff, a good man. Not perfect, but good."

Jeff pressed a gentle kiss into the hand on his cheek. Then he thought of Barry and Dr. Nerone. "What are we going to do about our two friends?' "

"What they did was at the best cruel and at the worst unprofessional, even criminal," Jeff said.

Tory sighed, "I know. I can't let Dr. Nerone get away with this."

"I know he won't." Jeff said.

"One thing though," Tory said. "I found out I'm a lot tougher than I thought."

Tory picked up Boby and wandered over the house, relishing the feeling of being completely relaxed and safe. She saw there was no totally safe place anywhere if the feelings of danger come from within.

Pausing in front of her roses, Tory looked in delight at the one in full bloom. It was pale salmon darkening to apricot in the center.

She whispered into Boby's silky fur. "We're home, Boby. I told you I'd get us home and I did, but I'll never be the same again. Like letting go of that window frame and starting down that dark road, I've made a giant step in my recovery. I've just got to keep on walking. This time I won't be alone, though. I'll have Jeff beside me. Not ahead, not behind, but as equal partners starting on a journey through the rest of our lives."

Jeff came to her then and held her close. "Can I still call you Tory or are you going to be Victoria from now on?"

Tory smiled impishly, "You can call me Tory, if you treat me like Victoria. If you slip up, I just won't answer you."

Journey

for Shirley
by Anita L. Pace

TRIP 1 - DESPAIR

I am lost
I am gone
Nowhere to be found
I am empty
I am sick
Afraid to get out

I am lying on the sofa
Hour after hour
Day after day
Hyperventilating, sighing
Only surviving

Every breath accounted for
Constantly gasping for air
Muscles clamping
Waves of panic
Please give me something to stop this Hell

My throat is saying it's forgotten how to swallow
Another former pleasure now denied
Enjoyment of feelings of fullness have left me
Nothing remains inside

You say it's only anxiety?!
You obviously don't know what it's like

A tumor, epilepsy, or perhaps a rare disease
But please don't tell me I'm really all right

I'd go to the doctor and get an exam
If only I could leave this place
The nearest hospital is two miles away
Can I get help in time
    before I start to die again?

Months have passed and I'm exhausted
The doctor said I'm fine
If this is how it feels to be healthy
How in hell does it feel to be dying?

I'm going outside for short walks now
Although I spin and sway
Back and forth on my street I struggle
Please, dear neighbor, don't stop to talk today

It's the night before my 27th birthday
In bed when suddenly aware
    I'm feeling nothingness
Have I finally lost it?
I jump in panic to prove I'm alive
(Whatever that means)

I'm waking to the pungent taste these days
Of undigested food on the back of my tongue
In strong defiance I hear it saying
"You've tried to swallow so much
    and that has been so wrong"

I've always done what I'm told I should do
Always have tried to be so damn good
I've taken great pains to do what is right
Am I simply destined for misery and strife?

I'm driving around my block more often
My body tense and steel
Bored to death with moving in circles
Despite the anguish I still feel

Other people can feel
    are real
They can visit, work, and drive
They can swallow their Valium
Not panic when they laugh
Oh, how I envy the Alive

April '79
I'm giving therapy another try
I'll learn how to laugh
Learn how to cry
Learn how to smile
And know why
I am

An appointment is made
April 30th, 4:00 p.m.
In the back of my mind lies the hope of a miracle
Relief in an hour of time

I sit and wait with a war
    inside
A room too white for eyes
My body is staying in spite of its shaking
My mind is shrieking "hide"

Your musical voice is calling my name
Your smile is sincere
    I think
You look rather nice
You look into me
I expected you to look at the ground

I stand and follow, my tension rising
You guide me to a door
What will I find beyond this outer space
On the journey to my inner core?

TRIP 2 - TESTING

The room is small
   but still I pace
Four feet is better than none
I'll sit on the table
I'll rock on the chair
But I can't get too close
So don't expect me to

Today I'm aching as I recall
   words in my baby book my mother once wrote
"She said 'bad girl' real clear today"
I was only 13 months old

I'm pressing against your wall in pain
I can't let you see the agony I'm in
My lungs beg to scream
My tears cry release
But my wall must remain to protect me

I want to trust you
But how can I trust
   a being as elusive as you?
I want to know first
   just what you're thinking
Convince me you care
   and then I'll start risking

When I asked if you laugh at me at home
I saw pained sadness strain your face
You said my name
   and said, "I don't do that"

I didn't really think you did

Something is changing
I'm hearing your words
Maybe you do
    mean what you say
So although feeling I've been getting nowhere
I'm sensing subtle movement toward my Way.

TRIP 3 - LEARNING

I seek all week
    to be with my Strength
Time can move so slow
So I do what I must
Do what is due
'til our day arrives again

I chew a pill
To take the drive
    that leads me to my Self
My stomach churns
    with burning excitement
To see my special friend

You've been teaching me lessons in the art of living
Guiding me patiently on the path to my Home
I'm becoming more aware of the powers I'm holding
I'm learning control comes in letting go

You showing me
    constantly
How life is full of paradoxes
For all that is true
    so is it's opposite
Self criticism is toxic
Things aren't always as they appear
It's been my own chosen thoughts

producing my fear

And women can be strong
It's okay to be wrong
Feelings are sensations we create
God won't punish me
    for feeling happy or angry
And only my life is my responsibility

There can be no love without pain
You remind me again and again
Whatever I feel is all right
Whomever I am, I am

Sixty minutes of nourishment
I feast on your presence and Light
I savor each moment
I sip your sweet wine
A healthy taste of fullness
In my very hungry time.

TRIP 4 - FEELING

Sometimes I want to curl at your side
My head on your lap as you sit
I think of the warmth of your gentle hands

    My child reaches out to you

Sometimes I want to walk with you
Taste your bitter and your sweet
Feel common grains of sand beneath our common
    feet

    My friend reaches out to you

Sometimes I want to work with you
Inspire and teach, guide and reach

Those searching for meaning in their lives
We'd spread more love in this love-starved world

My spirit reaches out to you

Sometimes I want to mother you
Take care of your needs
Save you from grief

My protector reaches out to you

Sometimes I want to yell at you
Sometimes I'm disappointed and hurt
I hate to get angry, but
Sometimes I do
Sometimes I forget that you're human, too

All my people within me are waking
Shaken by acceptance and care
You've shown me your strength
You've trusted in mine
When I have been angry
You have been kind

I'm choosing to live
I'm feeling happier
I'm choosing to risk
I'm feeling blessed
I'm pushing that dark cloud
    to another dimension
My hell is coming to an end.

TRIP 5 - LOVING

You were there when I needed someone
    to help me feel again
Someone to listen
Someone to care

Someone to let me need them
Without their getting scared

You were there
   when I reached out of my darkness
Not certain if I wanted to see
Unsure if I wanted to experience brightness
Unsure if I wanted to experience me

You were there
Everywhere
In my darkness
In my night
Through my pain
Through my fight

You were there to help me look into my own Light.

The Tools of Healing
by Franci Warner

Don't you just marvel at the courageous people you are reading about? Well, they are no different than you and I. They fought and fell down, fought again and got back on their feet. I compare ourselves to watching a boxing match; we fall down and get up over and over again, however painful it is.

I am 60 years old and have had p.a.'s (panic attacks) since I was 32 years old. Needless to say, 28 years ago is not like today. Psychiatrists knew absolutely nothing about our problem! (I take that back ... 28 years later, they are still not knowledgeable.) I went to a professional, who called it "nerves" for four years. I finally left disgusted. Being an inveterate reader, I began my own research and came across Dr. Claire Weekes from England who wrote three books. Her second, *More Help for Your Nerves* was the one that aided me in my climb. At least I knew what I had!

I worked all through those years of p.a.'s and inside knew I was slowly dying. I couldn't go anywhere without two beers. When I shopped, I'd stop at my local bar to have another. So I was "high" most of those years. When I worked, I took tranquilizers. Some days they got me through. Some days they didn't. So I decided to work in a bar for the next ten years and owned one as well. In that manner, I could drink when I felt a "what if" coming and no one would be the wiser in a drinking atmosphere.

At the age of 52 I had cancer. That changed my life. It is so sad to think that something that serious has to come about for change, but that bout made me think hard and long about my life. I made drastic changes and "divorced" many friends and family who were aiding my p.a.'s, not dissolving them. I learned how to speak up for what I believed in, no matter what the consequences were.

I slowly began to get well through internal healing. I threw my life on the floor like a giant crossword puzzle and began placing each piece back with clarity and thought. I stopped blaming others for what I had. It was so easy to place the blame somewhere other than myself. I viewed myself in those younger years and saw the decisions I made were based on other people's likes and dislikes. I saw for the first time that I was an adult with a child's mind. I was the perennial "people pleaser." Those two words wreaked havoc on me emotionally.

My steps were slow. The fear was abating on certain days, but on others it struck me head on. So I began to dissect those fearful times and found out that I had made a decision again based on pleasing others or someone had slighted me and I didn't retaliate. Slowly I began to take hold of my life. I no longer was fearful to speak up. I became assertive and took a stand for whatever I believed in, not caring, for the first time in my life, what others thought!

By removing those toxic people from my life, I began forming new friendships carefully based on encouragement and support. I no longer needed an army of friends, but one or two that were behind me at all times. I then began to work on my anger. To this day, anger is one of the keys to p.a.'s for me. We must clear up the past before we can go forward. How can we do this? By writing letters to the people who have hurt us. We don't have to mail them ... that's up to each of us. I sat down and hand wrote many letters and mailed none. But I spewed out all my anger and saw that in many incidences, I was to blame and not them. That is when I knew I was getting better. I stopped blaming and took responsibility for my own actions.

I stopped drinking ten years ago because I didn't need that support anymore. I was never an addictive person and never drank in the home nor over drank, but I always felt I needed that one or two to get me through my shopping days. I learned I had power that I had never used.

The hardest part was changing my negative thinking. I played a mental game with myself for years about "I should have, I could have, I would have." I stopped doing that. I told people how I felt instead of holding it in. If it meant a friendship gone by the wayside, it was too bad. I was the one who got up and went to sleep with fear ... they didn't. When I saw the world didn't cave in every time I spoke up, I continued to do it and still do. I vowed I would never allow another person to bring on a p.a. It's bad enough we do it to ourselves, but never again would an outside person aid me in an attack.

I began waking up differently. I shouted, "Thank you, God" every morning and still do. I understand how close I was to dying with cancer and how dare I not thank HIM for the day! I began writing down all my accomplishments, however small, on a piece of paper. Alongside I wrote down my negative thoughts for the day. By reading it every night, I saw I was making progress. I worked through my worst case scenarios if I had a p.a.

We know today after years of experience that we will not die, go crazy, have a heart attack or have to go to the Emergency Room. We also know that anxiety rises and peaks. So it was a matter of walking through that fear that was my answer. Because our memory banks are flooded with so much fear about having another p.a., we don't want to walk through the fear. We would rather avoid these situations. And so, many do just that. They narrow their world daily so as not to have a p.a. in an outside situation.

I was the Editor of a newsletter called The Mountain Climber, so named because of our long hard climb up the mountain. I began this five years ago because I was getting better and wanted to share my knowledge with others. I was scared to try such a risky venture and gave up my career as an Executive Secretary, a position I held for 20 years. Well, letters poured in and before you knew it, I was featured in Family Circle.

It's the risk that I took that changed my life. I became able to give back the knowledge I had garnered. But the most important point of wellness is risk-taking. Scary? You betcha! Had I not taken that chance to improve the quality of my life at 55 and a half years old, I would have never been able to climb the mountain as rapidly. Change and risk-taking are scary, but we are talking courage here and that is what I implore you to do; have courage and faith and things will work out. Our worst scenarios play in our heads daily, and yet they never occur. What precious wasted hours we have lost practicing "what ifs" instead of "so what's!"

Now I doubt whether you will agree with me, but through my clients, readers and personal experiences, I've learned that some of us deliberately keep our p.a.'s! We scream we'd do anything to not have them, but many of us keep them for our own subconscious desires. We might get more attention from certain members of our families or lover/spouse. Maybe in our youth, we never got the much deserved attention of a child. This might be our way of getting it. "Franci, you mean I shake and can't breathe and have so much fear and am doing it to myself?" Think about where you are in your life right now. Think about having no p.a.'s and what is expected of you. Can you do it? Okay, you have answered your own question!

You see, once free of p.a.'s through a magic pill that a scientist might invent, we become responsible for things we weren't responsible for before. That means shopping for ourselves again, returning the books to the library, taking the children to ballet and Little League, attending all the social functions we previously couldn't and on and on. So now do you understand that p.a.'s can become your friend as well as your enemy? The longer we hold on to them, the less responsibility and more attention we will get.

I have heard my readers and my clients (I hold private motivation sessions with individuals to learn how to keep the p.a.'s at bay) moan and groan about what they would be doing if they didn't have p.a.'s. Remember this, before you had them, can you honestly say that you didn't drink too much, smoke too much, do drugs, or eat too much? Can you say you had great relationships with family, friends, and lovers? The p.a.'s have stopped us from self improvement because our concentration is only on what ifs, the dreads, the heebie jeebies. So we must be truthful to ourselves and know that life wasn't a big blast before the p.a.'s entered our lives!

Know that all who read this book can be helped. How? From internal healing that comes from telling the truth to ourselves and stops us from blaming everything that happened in our life on others. We need to take responsibility for our own actions. Some of us came from miserable childhoods and it left its toll, but how long will we blame that childhood for the way we carry ourselves today? We must cut the past loose and concentrate on today. With all that pain from our past, we did learn something. We learned not to repeat actions of old. The saying is, "The first time, shame on you. The second time, shame on me!"

For those of you who are saying to yourselves, "I'll never be well again, I'll never do the things I did before," that is why you are not making steps. Picture your brain as a computer. Whatever you place in it causes a reaction. It has no feelings nor brain. And so when you place positive thoughts in there, you will be surprised at the results. You see, once you become aware of those negative thoughts, you will put up a stop sign immediately and refuse to place it in your computer. There are so many times when I began to think negatively and suddenly remembered the computer would pick it up. So I'd say, "Only kidding!"

It's important to remember that anyone who has had negative thoughts for years isn't suddenly going to stop. But awareness is the key. Once we become aware of what we are thinking, we can immediately switch to a positive thought. Also, when passing a mirror, smile! It doesn't matter what frame of mind we are in! When smiling it is difficult to have negative thoughts? Think about it!

These tools I have accumulated come from my own personal experiences as well as those of my readers and clients. I know what you might be thinking; "I read this book and feel good that others have conquered their fears, and today I am going to try to be more positive." Now day two comes over the horizon and there you go, forgetting all that you read. Well, that is normal and please don't be concerned about that lapse. Remember you have been geared to negative thinking so long that you can't be expected to walk around positive and happy. If you have to use this book as your "Bedside Bible" and read paragraphs from me and others who contributed their work, then do it. Take out affirmative sentences and place them on a card and repeat them to yourself as you begin and end your day. Highlight the sentences and paragraphs you wish to reread. Eventually your brain will be accustomed to positive thoughts.

"I am a failure" thinking is a problem. I know you say it every time you do something and can't continue it to its finality.

But a failure is someone who does not try! Please highlight this sentence because it is vital for your wellness! Take the example of going to the supermarket, for those who have difficulty with this. When you try to go there, you get in the car, you drive there, you enter, and then you stay there for awhile. But then you feel so badly if you have to leave even though you've achieved something! You did not fail! You showered, got dressed, made your list, got in the car, parked and entered, stayed and left. Look at all the accomplishments you made leading up to that. You tried and will try again another day. DO NOT browbeat and chastise yourself when you come home. "You idiot. You stupid. You wimp. You failure." Go over to that paper you are keeping and write down exactly what you did. You did not fail!

Another subject to be addressed is how we all want to do everything! People I work with want to never be afraid of anything again and chastise themselves because they can't fly yet or go on long vacations or get into an elevator. Well, let's hold up here! Do you think "normies" do everything? Stop anyone on the street and ask them what their fears are and you will need pages to fill it! Why do we think we have to do everything? Do you know I have people who stopped climbing the mountain and are very comfortable? Meaning, let's assume in your day, you have to do "x" amount of chores and you do it comfortably. You are happy staying alone in the house and have a rich full day. But you can't go on the freeway, so you take side streets. You have no intention of flying, and you walk up steps rather than take an elevator. So what!?

These people have determined that this is a safe life for them and quite normal because they can fill all theirs and their family's needs. A friend of mine used to be a music teacher. Over the years, her p.a.'s got worse. She resigned from the position, opened up a practice at home and is very happy. She isn't homebound, but is more comfortable working from her home. Fine! She does not have to go further. You must find out what you do in a day that fulfills you and others. If you can do that comfortably, then you don't have to climb higher up the mountain. You might say to yourself, "One day I think I will attempt one exit on the freeway," but don't bash yourself over the head saying, "I can't do that. What kind of scaredy cat am I?" In other words, it isn't a major thing and therefore it isn't vital to your wellness.

Our extreme thinking of trying to do everything is a waste of our energies and not fair at all to ourselves. We work on doing what makes us happy. If you have to work on certain things, then concentrate on that. The heck with the cruise and the five hour car trip. That will come later once you get more confidence. Each of us have agendas for the life we wish to lead. Concentrate on working on your own agenda.

Let's not forget about "what ifs." Say you get an invitation in December for your niece's wedding and it's now October. You begin to "what if" from October to December and the worst scenarios swirl in your head. Now think about that for a moment. Is it not the biggest waste of time to worry about something that isn't even happening? We all do it, but we must learn to stop it because worrying ruins an event months before it even happens. Those are "old tapes" playing again and we must remove them from our computer. So after getting the invitation and responding with a "yes," we need to put it out of our minds. About three weeks before the event, if it is nearby, we can do a "dry run." This is a wonderful tool. We can go to where the wedding is to take place, enter, and sit down. We can familiarize ourselves with everything, looking carefully about us and absorbing its beauty. We can learn the route so things look familiar the day we go. We can find the restrooms, the exits, and anywhere else we might be concerned about the location of. We've then eliminated the what ifs and are prepared to enjoy a great wedding.

I'm grateful for the opportunity to pass on my knowledge I've learned by experience over many years. Know that there are 19 million people who struggle with this every day. You are not alone. Get involved in groups or start one yourself. Reach out to others. Don't get selfishly wound up in you and only you. Giving of yourself is the answer to wellness. Start telling people you have anxiety so they will better understand what you are going through. Above all, have faith in your Higher Power and know that if you take the first step, HE/SHE will help you take the second.

Other disorders that can be associated with Panic Disorder

A person experiencing panic attacks should have a thorough physical examination because the symptoms can mimic other conditions as myocardial infarction, cardiac arrhythmias, hyperthyroidism, and certain types of epilepsy.

People with panic disorder may also suffer from clinical depression, substance abuse, obsessive-compulsive disorder, or irritable bowel syndrome.

Information provided by the National Institute of Mental Health (NIMH)

My Panic, My Life, My Recovery
by Rich Sterling

As a child, my life was one of apprehension and anxiety. I remember feeling anxious about swimming, traveling, or anything that involved being away from my parents for more than a day or so. I had a couple of panic attacks then but I didn't know what they were at the time. Anxiety lead to a stomach ulcer when I was seven. I felt phobic about going to school and my teachers were not understanding. Growing up, I knew that I was different because of the way I would accept or decline invitations to friend's parties and other events.

The panic finally caught up to me when I was in my mid-thirties. I was a young father with our third child on the way. I worked very hard as a teacher to keep up with a supervisor's relish for work and more work. I started to experience what I knew were panic attacks while I drove. Then one day shortly after arriving at work, my heart started to race. I was very psychologically and physically tired, feeling as if I were going to pass out. From that day on, I knew I had lost my strength to hold back the anxiety that had been my antagonizing companion for over thirty years. It was as if I could not hold that beach ball under water any longer.

Within three months my life completely changed for the worst. My wife was angry. My boss was angry. I was suffering with numerous panic attacks on a daily basis. I finally could no longer go to work. I became depressed and my doctor couldn't figure out what was wrong. Finally, in desperation after seeing a psychiatrist, my wife and I decided I needed more help. I spent a month in a behavioral health center. There I learned from others I was not alone. I had group sessions and individual sessions to help me learn new tools to a healthier life. However, this was also a time of personal hell for me. My wife wanted a divorce, my boss wanted to see me work or quit, the social worker did not understand panic disorder, and would belittle me for taking my medications the doctor had ordered. This person thought that one could only overcome panic disorder by flooding; to do what you fear the most until you panic and never retreat. Well, sorry to say, it just did not work for me.

What did work for me was to follow the advice of my psychiatrist and follow my routine of practicing driving, going out with family, shopping, and working. I returned to work but was constantly under the stress of more work than before. Between work and home pressures, I had one heck of a tough year on my hands.

I was fired from my job and found myself on disability. During that time, I took the opportunity and learned much about other approaches to overcome panic and anxiety. One that I still use today is visualization. I simply relax and go to one of several peaceful places in my mind. I envision all the elements around me and relax. If I am having difficulty with a person in my life, I bring them into the peaceful picture with me. He or she sits down with me and we talk. They leave and I can stay or leave. If it's an activity that I am having difficulty with such as traveling or shopping, I go to the peaceful place and then envision myself doing what I fear. I can drive around in my car alone and go places with greater ease each time I do this in the imagery of my relaxed state of mind. After doing this for a couple of weeks, my mind is so used to the event that it makes it much easier to do than if I had not.

I have also been hypnotized and have learned, through audio tapes, the art of self hypnosis. Now before you say, whoa, I can't and won't do that, listen. Visualization and hypnosis are really just a relaxed state of mind. We are more open to new ideas and more able to concentrate without anxiety in the way. Remember, you can be full of anxiety or relaxed. Not both at the same time.

I have a great psychiatrist who has worked with me to find the right medications to balance out my chemical imbalance that causes my panic. I also saw a psychologist who went out in the car with me to help me drive again. It was great to have such an experience, as it really jump started my driving again.

I belong to a very good panic/anxiety recovery group. We all help each other as we help ourselves. We have a network of members who we can telephone if we need to talk.

My wife and I found an experienced social worker in marriage therapy and we were able to regroup and rekindle our marriage.

To fill my time at home, I was on the daddy track with our three kids. I wrote a daily meditations book for those of us with the challenge of panic, but I was still bored. I knew that when I recovered someday, I would need to go back to work. This was a scary thought indeed. I'd break out in a sweat just thinking about it. So I looked into a nontraditional college education to earn my masters degree. I found a university that had a nonresident learning program and offered scholarships. I applied and wrote a great essay. I was awarded not just some scholarship money, but a full scholarship to earn my masters degree! That got me busy.

I still see a counselor who is a very understanding social worker. I practice expanding my world via driving, going to events, family outings and simply saying "Yes" to requests for help when someone calls and needs a volunteer. (I worry about how I am going to get there later if it's too far for me to drive that day.)

Today, I stand at the brink of recovery. When I look back at all the pain and anguish, I know that I have come a long way. I have new tools to help me through anything that I may encounter. I know that my higher power has a plan for me and that we so often take things like friends and family for granted. I know we are all special with much love and talent to share. Never let anyone tell you otherwise. Find a way to reach out and share your specialness with someone. It is your pathway to recovery.

Be good to yourself while on your journey.

Don attempts to alter his thoughts while flying.

The Pain Hidden Deep Inside
by Rochelle Krupp

As we neared the exit, I saw my mother-in-law. "Help me! I'm dying!" I screamed. She took me home and put me to bed where I stayed several days.

When I was six years old, our kindergarten class took a field trip to the St. Paul State Capitol. I remember being very excited, looking forward to my BIG ADVENTURE. When the special day finally arrived, my mom packed my lunch and off I went onto a large orange bus.

The Capitol was huge. I felt it would swallow me up. I walked to the top of the Capitol where beautiful golden horses attached to the building could be seen from an observation window. But as I walked to it, I suddenly became extremely frightened. I ran down all the steps to the bottom of the building and waited until my schoolmates returned. When they did, they all were talking about the beautiful golden horses.

I don't recall much more about my early years until the sixth grade. That's when we moved to a new city. I was the new kid in class, so I was constantly teased. Several times that year I sat with sweaty hands, a pounding heart, and a feeling as if I were going to black out and faint. I'd run to the bathroom as I discovered I could escape there when the scary feeling came. I learned early in life to keep my feelings and fears hidden deep inside myself. I was always the girl with the great sense of humor, laughing and acting happy, but I was very unhappy. Where did the pain go?

In junior high, I had a lot of uneasiness and became obsessed with my pulse. I spent my junior high years with my finger on my wrist, counting how many times a minute my heart was beating. In high school, I didn't go to any school events or anywhere else there were crowds. I didn't sleep at friends' homes or go to summer camp. I was terribly uneasy just thinking about those things. And I wonder, where did all that pain go?

I met my future husband in my senior year. We dated about a year before we started fighting. Bob became both physically and verbally abusive to me. I just accepted that our relationship was going to be that way. I usually apologized for any problems between us. I never cried or told a soul about what was going on. We got married in January of 1970. I was twenty.

One day I applied for a job at a large department store. The reception desk was on the twelfth floor. As I approached it, I saw blackness and felt faint. Petrified, I ran into the lounge. A high school friend walked up to me. Grabbing him, I pleaded, "Get me out of here!" We ran down all twelve flights of the escalator. I couldn't take the elevator down. As we neared the exit on the main floor, I saw my mother-in-law. "Help me! I'm dying!" I screamed. She took me home and put me to bed where I stayed for several days. As soon as I could, I returned to my job. But the "THING" happened again. I ran out of there shaking, never to return again. What was wrong with me?

I called my doctor who prescribed the tranquilizer, Librium. It didn't help me at all. I went to another doctor who gave me Valium. That pill kept me in bed for weeks. All I did was sleep and swallow Valiums. I felt awful all the time, still extremely frightened. I couldn't even stay alone in our apartment.

My family was supportive, but they had no idea what was wrong with me, either. I was a young bride of three months. Bob and I moved to an apartment closer to my parents and that seemed to comfort me a bit. I stopped taking the Valium and "white-knuckled" my way through the day. I stopped driving and wouldn't go anywhere unless accompanied by a family member. I considered them "safe." Even with support, I had a terrible time staying in stores or at anyone's home. I felt this "thing" was here to stay and there was no one to help me understand what was happening to me. The "thing" would rise and fall throughout the day. It would even wake me up in the middle of the night.

I got pregnant in 1972. For awhile, my marriage became less abusive. In the ninth month of my pregnancy, my husband locked me in a closet. When he unlocked the door, I climbed out of our bedroom window to get away from him. I gave birth to my son on June 5, 1973. I had a hard time staying in the hospital. My symptoms scared me there, too. Becoming a mom was a special experience for me and I loved my son as soon as I met him, but I couldn't even walk down the hall of the nursery to see him. I'd cradle him in my arms and wonder, "Why am I so scared?"

During those years, I visited one therapist after another. Not one of them seemed to understand anything about my problem. I saw social workers, psychologists, psychiatrists, internists, cardiologists, neurologists. Their pat answers were, "I don't know" or "It's your nerves." One psychiatrist I visited concluded that since Bob and I had only been married a short time and had a baby, we needed to keep working on our marriage. As for what was happening with my "nerves," he had no answer for me. When I asked him to go down the elevator with me, he said, "If you want to go down, go yourself!" I was petrified of elevators and hadn't been alone in one for years. This doctor had no clue about me, about my marital problems, or why I was so frightened of everything. I never saw him again.

My husband's job transferred him to Madison, Wisconsin, about a five hour drive from our home in Minneapolis. I packed up, believing our relationship would change in a new place and my "nerves" would get better. WRONG!!! Everything got much worse. I was scared all the time, experiencing terrible feelings of unreality, constant dizziness, difficulty in breathing, and I couldn't eat or sleep. I sat in bed all night shaking, feeling like I was losing my mind, or with any luck, dying!

The physical abuse ceased after our son was born, but the verbal abuse and degradation continued. My husband was only home on weekends because of his job. When he was home, he'd continually threaten to have me committed to a mental hospital. He said I was crazy. And I felt like I was, calling psychiatrists out of the yellow pages, crying hysterically for them to help me. One day I called my parents and begged them to pick me up and take me back home.

My son and I left Wisconsin and my husband. I felt like a zombie, laying in the back seat of my parents' car. By this time, I was afraid to leave the house and uncomfortable in the house. In my unending quest to get some relief from pain, I went to yet another doctor. This one gave me Equanil which actually calmed me a bit.

After six months, I rented a one bedroom apartment. My divorce became final in 1974 and I became free in one sense. But I was totally dependent on my family for everything: transportation, money, grocery shopping. My mother had a friend with a similar problem as myself. She suggested I get *Hope and Help for Your Nerves* by Claire Weekes. I finally had a name for what was going on with me and it's name was "agoraphobia." I wasn't going crazy. I wasn't going to die from it! Other people actually had this THING, too! Best of all, there was hope. I began seeing therapists again, but each new therapist would listen to my story and still not get it. I'd ask them to read Claire Weekes' book, but they'd all refuse.

I became friends with a woman in my apartment complex. I never told her about my problem. I never told anyone because I was so ashamed. But Sue knew I had limitations and that didn't seem to bother her. Thank God for Sue! We did everything together including the shopping, taking the kids to the park, and even swimming. I felt somewhat safe with her as long as I didn't overstep my boundaries. During this time I felt better than I had in a long while. I became less dependent on my family for my daily needs and had a friend for the first time in years.

Barry was an old friend. He came back into my life and we began dating. It wasn't easy. I tried working it so I'd be somewhat comfortable wherever we went. He made me feel special and we had a lot of fun together. For the first time, I felt I had a normal, honest relationship. But I hid the agoraphobia from him, too. When we got married in September of 1979, I was excited and happy. I loved this man! He was the finest person I'd ever met. We had a sweet, respectful relationship and I felt lucky. I went to work in his (our) company and enjoyed it, although I still experienced some anxiety. My life turned around and I felt like a totally different person.

In June of 1980, my dad stopped by. He said he wasn't feeling well. That concerned me because he'd had a heart attack the year before. My dad's doctor told me to get him to the hospital as soon as possible. I rushed to get my purse and my dad sat down on the couch. When I returned, he was in cardiac arrest. I screamed for my dad to speak to me. He'd always been there for me and now he needed me. What could I do? I called an ambulance.

Later the doctor told me that my dad had died almost immediately after sitting down and there was nothing I could have done. I'd loved this gentle, good, caring man so much and now he was no longer with me.

For years after his death, I had nightmares where I'd run away, screaming and crying. One night I stopped running. My dad walked up to me and said, "Don't be scared. I'm not going to hurt you. I'm sorry I scared you so much." After that night, my dad left my dreams and I haven't had another dream about him since. I never cried at his passing. Once again it was evident that I held onto my pain, never allowing it's release.

Six months after my dad's death, I was getting ready for bed when I had a full blown panic attack. Even armed with the knowledge I had, I couldn't control the awful feelings. I found a psychiatrist who told me he understood agoraphobia! He said I'd become re-sensitized by witnessing the death of my dad and gave me a new pill called Xanax. He said it would help control my panic and anxiety. Normally I was frightened of new medications, but I just swallowed the pill and didn't feel any side effects. I unwound a little and felt better.

My journey with Xanax had begun. Soon I wasn't as anxious and began to reclaim my life. I started helping my neighbor with the day care center she ran from her house. I really enjoyed the kids and loved making some money again. (I had had to stop working for our company.) I hated that I couldn't work with my husband, but working in the center gave me a sense of independence and helped me feel much better about myself. Life with my man, my work, and our kids (Barry had two from a previous marriage) was good. I was still not autonomous outside of my house, but my neighbor's house was nearly as comfortable as my own.

In 1983, we moved to a different house where I started my own day care business. I cared for 14 children and had two helpers. I loved the kids and what I was doing. We all had so much fun learning and playing. I continued with the Xanax and lived with a lot of limitations. For the most part, though, I did fairly well for awhile.

Then in May of 1987, I woke up feeling ill. I had cramps so I went to my doctor. He told me to take it easy for a couple of days as I was spotting. Two days later, a doctor from the clinic called. "Mrs. Krupp," he said, "you have uterine cancer." All I could say was, "Am I going to die?" He told me that if I had to have cancer, uterine was the most treatable. That night my doctor called and said he'd gone to look at the slides at the lab because I was too young to have this kind of cancer! Shaken and in shock, I called my psychiatrist. I asked if I could call him if I needed to and he said I could call whenever I wanted and that he would help me any way he could. I realized later that I told my psychiatrist about this before I even told my family.

I had to have a hysterectomy, about 28 radiation treatments, and then another surgery to insert a radiant implant that had to be in me for 72 hours. During those 72 hours, no one would be allowed in the room because of the radiation. No one! I went for a second opinion but was told the same thing. That was that, but how was I going to get through the next three weeks until surgery?

I closed my day care business the day I found out I had cancer. The parents weren't very happy, but I couldn't care for their children at this time.

I was brave. I kept my chin up, put a smile on my face, and went around all day like nothing was wrong. I'd learned this pattern well. At night, however, I laid in bed, terrified. Was it the cancer or was it what was expected of me in the coming months? How was I going to do this? Hospitals?! I don't do hospitals! Elevators?! No way! Radiation in a small room going through 28 treatments?! My mind was consumed with panic. I had a life threatening illness and I was afraid of the elevator ride! Now, I really thought I was CRAZY! I saw my psychiatrist who assured me I would rise to the occasion. AND RISE I DID!

I went for another opinion about the 72 hour radium implant. This doctor was located on the first floor ... where else? But when Barry and I got there, I realized that the first floor was really the third! I would have to go down two floors to get to the doctor.

We found the stairwell, opened the door, and then I froze. I wasn't going anywhere. We went to the lobby where I called the radiologist and begged him to meet me in the street level emergency room. "I have a department to run," he said. "I can't leave today. I'll meet you tomorrow, though." Bless him.

The next day we met in my "comfortable place." Unfortunately, the radiologist agreed with the procedures already planned for me, but I will eternally be grateful for his understanding. SHOW TIME!!!

I walked up to the surgical floor. From that point, I was in THEIR hands and what a handful they had! My mom was with me during the day and Barry came after work, staying with me through the night. I had someone with me around the clock. On the second day in the hospital, my doctor said that I didn't need the second surgery or treatments after all! What a relief! The third day he told me that the original plan was still on, but the good news was that the cancer had not spread. I turned into one big PANIC.

I called my psychiatrist and told him of my extreme anxiety. He said I could take as much Xanax as I needed. I was up to eight mg. a day, but felt no relief. Nurses came in and gave me other pills to calm me down. I'd pretend to swallow them, but when the nurses would leave, I'd spit them out, just like in the movies. Didn't they get it? I didn't trust any pills except Xanax.

New problem ... How was I going to get out of the hospital? I couldn't go down the elevator. I spent an entire day obsessing about the elevator with my fears running rampant. Barry and my mom managed to get on the elevator, but it sure wasn't easy. I have to give them a lot of credit because I can be extremely stubborn when it comes to my fearful places. As I was wheeled out of the hospital, I was so grateful that I nearly got down on my knees and kissed the ground.

My mom and I drove to Barry's car in the lot. I couldn't be without a "safe" person even in a hospital parking lot.

I had two weeks to recuperate at home before the radiation therapy was to begin. Fortunately, the radiation department had a private entrance and parking was available right outside the door. Everyday at 11:00 a.m., I'd go into a room and lay on a very narrow table that would raise up about five feet in the air while a massive machine would take its position working to save my life. I was terrified of the room, the noise, and knowing I couldn't move without the radiation going to the wrong part of my body.

One day I felt a lot of pain, so I had to see my gynecologist. The doctor asked me to lay on the table so he could examine me. Crying, I ran out of the room. I couldn't stay in there. I couldn't remove my clothes. I wanted out of that place!

No one knew what to do. The nurse spoke with me. I agreed to use the ladies room in the lobby of the clinic where she'd take the samples she needed. During this time all I could do was go for treatments and then return home. I was totally re-sensitized and felt as if I could not cope with anything. I was in a full-blown setback. My agoraphobia had never been so severe.

In October I went through the second surgery. I made arrangements with the hospital staff to stay in a hospice room so my mom and Barry could stay in the adjoining room. Although they could not come into my room, at least I could call them. I couldn't sleep for the three days I was there. I was so anxious and overtired that when the radium implant was removed, I actually allowed a nurse to give me a sleeping pill. The minute I woke up, I flew out of there! (I vowed to never again return to a hospital and to this day I've kept that vow.)

Recovering from those six months was my next step. Physically, I was extremely weak and exhausted. I increased the Xanax and tried to rest and regain my strength. I started slowly to attempt leaving my house with my mom, but I was so phobic that I couldn't. After many tries, we finally got to a park at the end of my block. I could stay for only a few minutes before bolting home.

A friend told me about a tape program she'd heard about. This program included weekly informational tapes, journaling, meditation tapes, and homework assignments. The program was helpful but I couldn't listen to the meditation tape the ten times a day I was expected to. I dropped out of the program.

I bought every book on the subject of agoraphobia, panic, and anxiety that I could find. I started working very hard on my recovery, as well as no longer willing to be the non-assertive person I'd always been. I was determined to get this agoraphobia out of my life more than ever. I wanted to lay under a machine and have it take it away just as the one that killed those deadly cancer cells. But no such luck. It doesn't work that way.

Working on the trip to the park with my mom took about three months. Even then, I could only stay a short time. I tried to get into a grocery store I'd frequented almost daily before my illness, but I couldn't get past the front door. The door had a bench by this door so mom and I would just sit there and watch people come and go. Why couldn't I do that? It was just a store.

My goal was to get a carton of milk located at the rear of the building. It took me eight months, but I got my milk! My boundaries were very small, but I kept plugging along, extremely patient with myself. I practiced day after day. Some were easier than others.

My doctor told me of a support group for agoraphobics. "Rochelle," he said. "Your agoraphobia is more of a problem than your cancer was." I went to the group meeting but experienced so much panic that I had to leave. So I asked the leader if the group could meet at my house and she agreed. They held their next meeting at my home, but I never saw them after that! A few days later a woman called to say that she had missed the meeting, but had heard about me. She called to introduce herself because she was a fellow phobic. I'd never met another agoraphobic before attending the group, so this call was very important to me.

The woman's name was Ruth. Before long, we became close phone friends, spending a lot of time together talking, sharing, and laughing. Barry and I often visited her and her husband in her home and we all got along fine. But four years into our friendship, I discovered Ruth was an alcoholic. When I realized how severe her problem was, I contacted each member of her family and pleaded with them to get help for her.

Ruth did enter a two week treatment program and came out clean and sober. She also seemed to be free of phobia symptoms. So guess what? Ruth dumped me as a friend.

So there I was again, alone with my agoraphobia. I sought out therapist after therapist. None of them were willing to go out "into the marketplace" with me. I finally went back to the psychiatrist who introduced me to Xanax. After ten years, he was still willing to meet me in the cafeteria at the medical center. I expressed to him my frustration and asked for any help he could give me. That began my long and bumpy road with antidepressants.

I took the first such pill he prescribed for six weeks. One morning I woke up not knowing who I was! I was totally confused! After that I tried almost every antidepressant available, but couldn't tolerate the side effects. Or were they? Like many agoraphobics, I am also medicine phobic. It's difficult for me to know if I'm having a REAL side effect or have talked myself into one. Since I'm careful to read up on all the side effects, the chances are that I might sometimes cause them myself.

Whether real or imagined, I learned I could not tolerate antidepressants. I do have some true allergic reactions to some medications since my hysterectomy and that has confused me more. I think most doctors just don't get it. They can't grasp the fact that people can be so medicine phobic that they refuse to take a pill that has the potential to aid them in their recovery. I'm still searching for a pill, besides Xanax, that I can tolerate.

I finally met Rae, a fantastic therapist. Her office was a revamped house only one mile from my house. Rae worked with me to help me find my soul. She led me to a spiritual road I'd never known existed. She said that I was like a sparrow with a broken wing. We worked together to heal me. We talked about my phobias, but she also wanted me to look deep inside myself to find the two things that were so important to healing ... peace and joy. I began to meditate. It took a lot of practice because my mind learned to concentrate, but my body was so tense all the time it was hard for me to relax. So Rae encouraged me to visualize peaceful things that brought me joy and beauty. She wanted me to rid myself of the poison in my life ... people who I had allowed to treat me badly. She taught me how to deal with my pain and taught me I didn't deserve the terrible things I'd endured.

I learned to show my emotions more. I began expressing anger, hurt, and frustrations. Most of all, I began learning how to FEEL. Rae was the only therapist I'd seen who had read Claire Weekes' book, *Agoraphobia* (which I think was her best book.) Rae also had cancer 17 years before we met, so we could talk about how much fear my cancer had caused me as well as how badly it had re-sensitized me.

Two years into our therapy, Rae sat me down and told me she had cancer again. This was the first time she saw me shed a tear. I loved her so much. Now she was the sparrow that needed to heal. We saw each other for one more time as she was going to put all her energy into healing herself. (As of this writing, Rae is doing very well and I pray for her complete recovery.) I owe her so much. She taught me about all the beauty in the world. She opened me up to all the kindness, joy, peace, and love that surrounds me.

Where could I go from there? I called Judy, the leader of the support group for agoraphobics, and asked her to do "in-vivo" work with me, (taking people into the world and helping them deal with their panic as it happens).

This work has helped me tremendously on my road to recovery. Judy is a recovering agoraphobic and coauthor of the book, *Embracing the Fear*, a cognitively oriented book that deals with agoraphobia, panic, and anxiety disorders. She started her support group, The Open Door, in 1986. My motto is "It takes an agoraphobic to understand an agoraphobic."

Our first appointment was at my house. Judy and I talked about the goals I'd made for myself. We made an appointment to go out the next week. We started by going a mile to the east and a mile to the west. Believe me, it wasn't easy! Judy and I have been working together for two years. We have one appointment a week during the school year, and since Judy is a teacher, we can have up to three sessions a week during the summer.

In the last two years, I've practiced going in malls, restaurants, universities, and even the Mall of America which is four million square feet big. Granted, my feet have not touched all of the four million square feet, even with my size ten feet, but I bet I have strolled several thousand! We've been almost everywhere in my city of Minneapolis and have also visited St. Paul. We cruise!

Judy and I have taken mini-road trips as far as an hour away from my house. I went on an overnight retreat with her. She had to share a room with me. So what if she got no sleep?! We shop, shop, shop. I'm beginning to become autonomous for short periods of time when I am with her. Autonomy is my long term goal. When the day comes that I have reached this goal, I hope we can still play. She's been so much fun for me, even in my terror.

Everyday I do something on my own whether practicing walking around my neighborhood or driving, which I prefer. I get out of the house everyday with a "safe" person. My middle name has become PRACTICE. I must be a slow learner because it was only a few years ago that I realized it wasn't *the place I was afraid of, but how I would feel in that place.*

All of the dozens of therapists I visited over the years didn't specifically help with my agoraphobia. When I reflect back, though, I now know they all taught me something to help me build a healthier personal foundation. Some of the things that I find helpful when out in the world are: always having water with me, carrying affirmation cards on a ring that I can refer to when I become anxious, and going to places prepared to feel whatever I'm going to feel. I also try to change my "what ifs" to "so whats." I can now say that I am on the correct road to recovery and am willing to flow with whatever comes my way. The ups and downs of agoraphobia. What a roller coaster ride!

I was motivated to write my story by a very dear friend who also suffers with agoraphobia. She persuaded me that my story was worth sharing. I can see now that writing this story is part of my recovery process. I've put my secret life down on paper which proves to me I've left my shame behind. Thank you, Susan Turner, my dear friend and practice partner, even though we live many states and thousands of miles apart. Although we may both fear "planes, trains, and automobiles," Susan and I know we will meet someday.

Believing in Myself
by Jane

I grew up in an alcoholic home, basically being the one in the family that took care of everything and everyone's needs. I didn't mind, though. I felt it was my responsibility in some way.

Love wasn't given or shown in my family. We were considered terrible if we felt angry or sad, or had any other emotion for that matter. It just wasn't right to talk about feelings. Nothing was talked about. Nothing at all.

I was in the third grade when I first experienced panicky feelings. I'd been sick one night. When I went to school the next day, I thought, "What if I throw up in front of someone or in class?" The "what ifs" started and I left school every day at recess for at least a week or two.

I had it in my mind that I should be ashamed or embarrassed if something happened that I couldn't control. I only wanted to play at my house, never feeling comfortable playing at someone else's. But even though I had what I would call "social phobia," I later managed to participate in volleyball, soccer, basketball and track. I was even the pitcher on a very good baseball team. These activities put me in the public eye, terrifying me for the first five minutes. But then I'd get so involved that I'd forget to be scared anymore.

When I finished high school, I felt relieved because I thought I'd never again have to face those awful anxious feelings. Why should I since I'd never have to sit in a classroom again? But how wrong I was. I got out into the work place and had to deal with people all the time. And that scared me to death. It was strange, though, because I liked people and think I'm very good with the public. It didn't make sense.

I had several jobs. Cashiering was extremely stressful because I had to wait on people. I later worked as a delivery driver which was fun. But when I hurt myself and couldn't lift much anymore, I had to quit.

At the same time, I was in a relationship with the same person for a few years. That person was another woman, a fact which brought up a great deal of anxiety in itself. I didn't feel I was "gay," but I did fall in love with this woman. Amy and I had been best friends and played sports together. And when I turned 21, I moved out of my parents' house and in with her. We both worked full time and bought a beautiful mobile home after one year. I felt it was our first home together, but the feelings of anxiety remained. I had conflicts about my feelings for men and wanted the marriage part as well as being able to be openly together in public. But I couldn't have that with another woman.

Amy and I lived in this home for five and a half years before putting it up for sale to buy another house. I kept asking myself if that was what I truly wanted. Did I want to spend my life in the gay lifestyle? Should I get married? Did I want to have kids? These thoughts stirred through my mind.

I'd bought a brand new truck that I'd saved up for years to buy. I was driving to my parents' house one day when suddenly I couldn't breathe and got dizzy. I started hyperventilating and nearly lost control of my truck. The physical sensations terrified me, worse than any experience I'd ever had. I didn't know then that this was my first panic attack.

I finally made it to my parents' house, but I couldn't move from the truck at first. My legs were weak. I waited five minutes, then went in, having no idea what had just happened. I felt I couldn't say anything to my parents because their reaction would've been that I was crazy. Amy and I decided to not buy a new house yet.

This was a busy time in my life. I had a couple of cleaning jobs and went to school to study computers because I didn't know what I wanted to do with my life. But I felt that I wanted to be able to say I was this or that; something I could be proud of. I also began working as a meter maid three days a week. Talk about stress! Everyone hated me because I gave them tickets. Even some of the police officers said my job was harder than theirs. It didn't help when I got sent to a huge department store to pick up items for the office. I noticed I hated waiting in lines and found it near impossible to do so.

Two friends died around this time, one by suicide. That's when I began having p.a.'s at work. I felt overwhelmed and thought I'd feel better if I let go of some of the stress in my life, so I quit one cleaning job I had. Then I quit school.

But instead of relaxing, I had my worst panic attack I'd ever experienced while working. It happened during my shift as a meter maid. I was so petrified that I ran out the door and drove home. To this day, I have no idea how I got there safely. My world quickly shrunk smaller and smaller.

My brother and I were best friends at the time ... or so I thought. I told him about the panic attacks and he told me that his life was so happy that he didn't want to hear about my depression. How nice, especially from a guy who'd gone through a divorce three years earlier and had moved in with me for six months. There was no support. Had I asked for money, he would've been there. But emotional support was something he wasn't capable of giving.

I became stuck at home except for the one to two miles I could get away with Amy. It was a horrible and depressing time for me. I joined Mel Green's *New Beginnings* home program and that helped somewhat. Mel was such a good friend to me when no one in my family was there. But Amy turned out to be my best friend. I finally realized that she must love me a lot to not walk out on me the way that I was.

Six months after becoming agoraphobic, I got physically ill. I called my doctor, and from my symptoms he thought I might have appendicitis. I told him there was no way I could come in. It'd been six months since I'd been that far away from home. His nurse told me that if I didn't get to the hospital, she was going to call an ambulance. I reluctantly took a small dosage of Xanax that a friend had given me before. Amy drove me to the hospital.

My pulse was 156 when I arrived. I told the doctors and nurses about my panic attacks and they were very nice to me. After three hours, they discovered a cyst on my right ovary. As strange as it might seem, this event became the turning point in my life. I felt I could do anything after making it to the hospital and through the procedures, so I went to see my parents. They were surprised and happy. My dad actually hugged me.

Two months later, I saw a psychiatrist who verified what the therapist had told me; I had panic disorder. He gave me a prescription for Xanax and I began treatment with him.

It was one and a half years ago that I became extremely limited. During those six months, I read all I could about p.a.'s. That helped me believe a panic attack wouldn't kill me. I still have the same prescription for Xanax because I choose to work on myself without medication whenever possible. However, I carry the pills with me wherever I go. I see a doctor who specializes in biofeedback, teaching me to teach myself to relax. He's also helping me with my sexual identity conflict.

I work on my driving alone daily. I've learned that when I face something difficult and accomplish it, the better I feel about myself. I can now go anywhere with Amy. We recently took a 2300 mile trip to South Dakota and it was wonderful. I was so happy with myself for making that trip possible. I also did all my own Christmas shopping this year which made me feel good about myself. I still have problems waiting in lines at stores and driving alone, but I am working on becoming more independent all of the time. And when the panicky feelings come, I try to flow through them, knowing that I will be all right.

I'm on the road to recovery, even if I still have many hurdles to climb. We all can recover, but we need to support each other. I've much support from pen pals, far more than from family members. My friends and I encourage each other to continue ahead. And sometimes I think I work on myself too much and forget to have fun. I've learned you can't always take life so seriously. You've got to have some fun, too.

I read all I can by Louise Hay. She's helped me more than anyone to like and love myself. I now see how growing up feeling bad just for existing has made it important for me to start life all over in ways, changing ideas and behaviors. I've learned, too, that I'm not responsible for everyone's feelings and that it's not my responsibility to take care of everyone's needs. I am, however, responsible for taking care of mine. And as I do, my anxiety lessens and I am happier.

Hope After Illness and Agoraphobia
by Marie Anderson

At age 23, I was under a great deal of stress and did not feel well. It was during this time that my grandmother was taking care of her husband who was dying from cancer. She commented on how difficult it is on others when a person is ill and said it'd be better for her if he died.

I was also pregnant with my youngest daughter. My former husband and I were at the movies one evening when I began feeling nauseated. I thought he'd be understanding. Instead, he told me how awful my face looked when I'm sick.

My grandmother's and ex-husband's comments made permanent impacts on me. From then on, whenever ill, I wanted to hide in my bedroom and be alone. Having experienced a lot of rejection in my life, I'd already felt unworthy.

"What if I get sick while I'm out with someone?" I began worrying. "What will they think of me?" Meanwhile, other long term family problems continued, but I hadn't realized how these anxieties were causing many of the symptoms I was feeling.

My pulse raced. I had difficulty breathing. I felt faint. I went from doctor to doctor, but no one could find a thing wrong with me. It was unnerving because these "attacks" came out of the blue. I never knew when "it" could happen and the lack of a doctor's diagnosis only made it worse. What would people think of me, I wondered? Probably that I was crazy.

I gradually restricted how far away from home I went and stayed there most of the time, often in bed. It's difficult to maintain friendships when you can't function well and it was even difficult for me to have people at my house for fear I'd have an attack while any visitor was there. I did not want anyone to see me like that and I needed to be alone. I needed to relax. So there went any social life.

I do love to read, however, and I found a self-help book at the store. I skimmed through it and found an explanation of agoraphobia. I was shocked because it sounded just like me! The book told of an organization called TERRAP. I called and they sent me a questionnaire. This confirmed the diagnosis. I finally knew a name for what I had.

There was no way I could go to a treatment center, so I took the home correspondence course. I learned many things like relaxation and distraction techniques, as well as the damaging effects of "what if" thinking and worrying about what other people think. I spoke to a psychologist on the telephone for awhile. He helped me to sort out certain family issues as well as identify false beliefs learned at an early age. One such belief was believing things that went wrong were my fault.

In addition, I read some of Dr. Robert Schullér's books because they are so positive. I especially liked *You Can Be the Person You Want to Be*. I also saw the benefits of good nutrition. I know I feel better when I eat right and so I did. And I walked to relieve stress.

I improved a great deal, but then I became very ill. This set me back. It took a year for the doctors to diagnose the problem and the eventual surgery corrected it. Recovery was slow, but I never reverted to where I was before understanding agoraphobia. I learned that it's much easier controlling anxiety when feeling well.

I wanted to make a better life for myself and my children. I'd always wanted to attend college, but had feared I wouldn't be able to because of my health problems and the agoraphobia. "What's the worst thing that can happen?" I asked myself. My answer was that I'd get sick and not be able to do it. I decided to apply, telling myself all I can do is try my best. If I quit, at least I'd know I'd made the attempt. I'd take one day at a time, one test at a time. "It doesn't matter if you succeed or not at something you attempt to do," I'd always told my daughters. "You're a winner just because you tried." Now I said these things to myself.

I entered a local community college. All through school in every class, I sat as close to the door as I possibly could. Giving oral reports were especially difficult because of my fear of having an anxiety attack for all the class to witness. So I practiced relaxation and distraction techniques while countering negative self-talk with positive thoughts.

My last year was especially challenging. I needed a hysterectomy. Heavy bleeding caused me to feel faint and weak. In my very last class I just couldn't force myself to give the oral reports and the instructor gave me an incomplete. I'd have to wait one year until the class was offered again.

I had the surgery immediately after the school term ended and I finished the class the following Spring semester. I felt well enough to control my anxiety and give my two speeches to complete the class requirements.

I graduated with two Associate in Arts Degrees with Highest Honors and the Academic Excellence award for Sociology. I transferred to a four year college where I received my Bachelors and Masters of Science degrees.

As well as the success of completing school, I loved the help I was able to give others when I performed my practicum as a community college counselor for a year and a half. There were two instances where a student would've quit school due to anxiety and panic had I not intervened. One student's anxiety during tests was so high that she had to leave class. I helped arrange with her professor for her to sit outside during tests so that the instructor could see her while the other students could not.

The other student had severe anxiety in Speech class, like myself, and giving these speeches were mandatory in order to pass. I explained the stress response to her and taught her relaxation techniques. She completed the class with an "A!"

I faced another challenge when my youngest daughter became pregnant and wanted me to be her coach, along with her sister. I desperately wanted to be there for her, but I wasn't sure I could be. So I took the pressure off myself by thinking that her sister would be there so that she wouldn't be alone, no matter what I did. My daughter went into labor at 4:00 a.m. one morning. I called her sister to meet us at the hospital. What a pair we were! My daughter was in pain and I felt like I couldn't breathe! At the hospital we were surprised to find the door locked. Using another entrance meant being further away from my car. I tried to not focus on that and had my oldest daughter drive my car closer to this other entrance when she arrived. That helped me relax a bit.

During my daughter's four hour labor, I had to leave the room once to relax. But I was present to enjoy the thrill of witnessing the birth of my beautiful grandson!

My biggest challenge these days is caring for this precious 10 month old grandchild while his mother attends college. I feel safe while caring for him because I have my daughter take a beeper with her in case I need to contact her. Knowing I can call her no matter where she is, is a great comfort. This is her second semester and I've never had to call her out of a class.

I want to close with the story of a recent event. My oldest daughter lived at UCLA while a student there. It's about a 45 minute drive from my home. I visited her at her dorm for about five minutes a couple of times when she first began attending there.

Then I felt unable to visit her for more than three years. I kept in touch by calling and by letters, but it broke my heart not being able to see her on campus and attend mother/daughter events. As her June, 1994 graduation grew nearer, I felt my desperate desire to be there for her. I knew how much she wanted me to attend, yet being the sweet person she is, she put no pressure on me. She said she'd understand. I began practicing the drive to Pauley Pavilion where the ceremony would take place. And I prayed I'd feel well on graduation day.

When the day arrived, I got in the car with my youngest daughter and my grandson. I told them I didn't' know if I could do it, but I was going to give it a try. I made it to the parking lot. Then I looked across the bridge I knew I'd have to walk over and saw how far I'd be from my car. I felt concerned but I kept telling myself I could do it.

And I did. The next challenge was the sight of the hundreds of people waiting to get into the building. I wanted to sit by the door and was gratified that most people were more concerned with sitting up front! I got to sit in a perfect spot where I felt comfortable.

The procession of graduates began. So many students filed in that I wondered if I'd ever spot my daughter in such a crowd. My youngest daughter saw her first. (It didn't hurt that she was the only one wearing red high heels!) We watched as she turned around in a complete circle, her eyes searching the crowd, wondering if her mom had made it for her big day.

The first time she looked our way, she didn't see us. The second time, I stood up and put both my arms in the air, waving at her. Suddenly her eyes met mine and the biggest, happiest, smile came across her face! I will never forget that moment for as long as I live.

At 40 years of age, I'm still on the road to recovery. It's been bumpy, especially since I've had so much illness to deal with. But I've experienced precious moments along the way that I would have missed had I not improved over the years. I recall my struggles at 23 and I see how far I've come, enjoying life more and more, getting better and believing full recovery is possible.

What is the treatment for Panic Disorder?

Once diagnosed, panic disorder is highly treatable. Appropriate treatment can reduce or completely prevent panic attacks in 70-90 percent of patients, especially when diagnosed early.

In 1991, a conference held at the National Institutes of Health (NIH) surveyed the available information on panic disorder and its treatment. It was concluded that cognitive-behavioral therapy and medications are both effective for panic disorder. Treatment should be selected according to the individual needs and preferences of the patient and any treatment that fails to produce an effect within 6-8 weeks should be reassessed.

Information provided by the National Institute of Mental Health (NIMH)

Panic, No Longer
My Constant Companion
by Gerry Kulpa

I remember feeling very nervous as a child whenever I had to face something unfamiliar. I'd get headaches and stomachaches the day before a test. My knees would shake and my heart pound if I had to speak in front of the class.

I recall sweaty palms, palpitations, and feeling faint before job interviews. But I begin my story when I first realized what a true panic attack is all about.

In the early 1970's, I was 20 years old, newly married, and working full time as a secretary. I felt relatively happy and enjoyed my life as a wife, living away from my parents for the first time.

But problems began in our second year of marriage. My husband lost his job and I had to support both of us. Besides outside work, I cleaned the house and did the shopping and laundry while my husband partied day and night. It wasn't long before he got involved with another woman. I was devastated.

In an attempt to save our marriage, we moved to Arizona. My husband found work right away, but I did not. I didn't know anyone and called my family often. It was during this time that I had my first panic attack and I was scared.

I couldn't bear being away from everything familiar to me, so I flew home at my first opportunity. With my marriage remaining in trouble, I moved back to my parents' house with nothing but the clothes on my back. And I began having panic attacks all the time. I couldn't sleep. The sound of my own heartbeat was deafening. I was certain I was losing my mind.

My mother took me to our doctor who gave me tranquilizers and sleeping pills. At this point I was almost completely housebound, not even able to go into the yard without having a panic attack.

After a couple of months, I struggled back to the doctor because I wasn't getting any better. He told me, point blank, that if I didn't straighten myself out, he'd have to put me in a mental hospital. I was shocked and petrified at that prospect.

I made a decision that day; I would make myself well. I'd read an advertisement for a book on nervous illness called "Hope and Help for Your Nerves" by Dr. Claire Weekes. I sent for it and read it from cover to cover, learning what was wrong with me. I had a nervous illness brought on by extreme stress. And I was not alone.

My recovery began by going outside and sitting on a lawn chair for a few minutes each day, gradually increasing the time. I'd had difficulty swallowing food, but I forced myself to eat.

Within a few more months, I borrowed money from my parents to look for a used car so I could get a job. My cousin took me to look at an old Volkswagen at a local gas station. He knew the mechanic and said he'd make me a good deal. I didn't know at the time that this was a prearranged meeting so that the mechanic could ask me for a date. Determined to begin a new life, I accepted the date.

George and I spent a lot of time together. He knew all about my nervous illness and helped me get off the pills. He also helped me find an attorney so I could begin divorce proceedings as I was still married.

But then just two weeks before my court date, I was alone with my mother when she had a heart attack. The ambulance rushed her to the hospital, but within twenty minutes she was dead. I was crushed.

My father was working on a tug boat and I had to notify him via the Coast Guard to return home. I only had him told there'd been a family emergency. But at the train station I told him the horrible news. I was in a state of shock for the next several days, and my old friend "Panic" returned.

I was a nervous wreck when I went to court for my divorce. With the help of a wonderful woman security guard, I managed to get through the proceedings. While the guard stood in the back of the courtroom, she had me focus on her as I answered my attorney's questions.

A few months after my divorce became final, and two years since I'd met George, we got married. I felt happy again. We did everything together. George wanted me to stay at home and have children. I was content to do so and had my first child at 26 and my second six years later.

Then George's job changed and he had to travel quite a bit. He was gone for weeks at a time, but I managed with the help of my father. George's time away put a strain on our marriage, but I was determined to make this marriage work. We moved a few times over the years, but hard as I tried, our problems got worse. George became very controlling and jealous of everyone who came in contact with me, especially when he was on business trips. We fought all the time over the kids. I realized, too, that I'd become extremely dependent on him.

In 1987, George's mother became severely ill with cancer. I volunteered to take care of her in our home because she didn't want to die in a hospital. I nursed her for about six months until she passed away. It was an emotionally exhausting time for all of us and the panic attacks returned again ... but only for a short time and not as severe as before.

Then in 1991, my father got pneumonia. I visited him every day in the hospital, but he kept having more and more complications. After nearly three weeks, he died. I felt crushed again, but this time I didn't panic. Instead, I felt deep sadness. My only brother and I had to take care of all the legalities and I think that keeping busy helped me through this ordeal.

And now comes the hard part. I dealt with my divorce, my mother's death, my mother-in-law's illness and death, and my father's death. But just eleven months after my father died, my husband also passed away. He was on a business trip at the time. The doctor told me he'd done all he could to save him. I felt shocked. I just couldn't believe George had died. It seemed my whole world was collapsing in on me. I had no idea what to do and how I was going to get through this loss.

The next few weeks were a blur. For months I dealt with paperwork and everything else that came up. And then about a year later, the panic attacks began again. My doctor gave me a complete physical and discovered my cholesterol was high, so I started a low fat and low sugar diet, losing 17 pounds and lowering my cholesterol level. But the panic attacks continued. My doctor then prescribed Prozac. The panic became much worse, so he had me stop it. Then he prescribed Xanax. That seemed to help a little, even on a mild dose.

I decided to consult a psychologist. It was difficult for me to go regularly because I was becoming agoraphobic again. I continued for several weeks, but financial considerations made it impossible for me to continue. My regular doctor told me I'd have to stop taking Xanax because of state regulations. I was very reluctant to try something else, so I decided to gradually cut down the dosage and stop taking it altogether.

I found a support group in the newspaper, but the meetings were further away than what I thought I could drive to. The leader of the support group gave me the name of a woman who lived near me and I was able to ride with her a few times. Even that became too difficult, so the leader arranged a phone counseling session once a week. She sent me information on newsletters and other materials relating to panic attacks and agoraphobia. I subscribed to Straight Talk and ENcourage and began writing to pen pals. I ordered books and tapes which proved helpful. One tape that describes most of the symptoms associated with panic attacks helped put my mind at ease about a particular symptom that scared me a lot.

Pen pals have become a very enjoyable interaction. Since all of the people I correspond with are either currently suffering from this illness or recovering from it, I find these pals to be a great source of comfort and support. I've found that getting involved in things I enjoy is a great distraction.

In the Fall of 1993, I stopped taking Xanax. While it helped me for awhile, I was concerned it was making me more depressed. I used vitamins for awhile, but they didn't seem to agree with me. I do avoid sugar and eat lots of fruits, vegetables, and low fat foods. For exercise, I use a treadmill when I can't walk outside.

I don't have much family left to depend on, so I'm learning to cope on my own for the first time in my life. I discovered through experience that I easily lose confidence in myself when the fear of a panic attack begins to take over my life. One way I've found to help overcome this is setting goals and finding ways to accomplish them. I try to not get discouraged, even if I think I've failed. Then, as more goals are accomplished, confidence returns and the attacks diminish in severity and frequency.

I haven't worked outside the house for many years, but I'm taking a home study course on Medical Transcription. Although it's difficult to concentrate at times, I keep trying. I'm 45 years old as I write this and have two teenage children. I look forward to the day I can say I am fully recovered. In the meantime, I consider myself recovering, trying new things, searching for that which gives my life more enjoyment.

What About Medications?

Several classes of medication can reduce or prevent panic attacks and decrease patients' anticipatory anxiety about having attacks. The medications most often used are: antidepressants, including tricyclics, monoamine oxidase inhibitors, serotonin reuptake inhibitors, and certain high-potency benzodiazepines. Choice of drug to use is based on safety, efficiency, and personal preferences of the patient. Dosages generally begin low and are built up. This procedure often minimizes side effects.

Treatment with high potency benzodiazepines effectively reduce anxiety. Alprazolam (Xanax), clonazepam, and lorazepam belong to this class. They take effect rapidly and are well-tolerated by most patients. Some patients may become dependent on benzodiazepines, especially those who have had problems with alcohol or drug dependency.

MAOI's require the patient to observe exacting dietary restrictions because certain foods and other prescription drugs and substances of abuse can interact with the MAO inhibitor and cause a sudden, dangerous rise in blood pressure.

Editor's Note: Treatment by medication may be hampered if the patient has severe drug sensitivities or a medicine phobia.

Information provided by the National Institute of Mental Health (NIMH)

Got More to Do Than
Sit on My Porch
by Lindsay Sonia

It was April of 1991. I was 14 years old, sitting on my porch, when I experienced one of the scariest moments of my life. It lasted only about fifteen minutes, but it felt like hours.

I felt my throat closing. It got tighter and tighter until it seemed I couldn't breathe. Then I felt like I was going to vomit. My knees trembled and my world began to spin. I felt hot, then cold, then hot again, cold, hot, cold ... back and forth. I could hear and feel my heart as it seemed to beat out of my chest. Boom! Boom! Boom! I saw black. That's all I saw.

With all this happening at once, I thought I had to be dying, so I ran to my mother and told her exactly how I felt. She immediately knew what I had because the same thing happened to her sometimes. She took me to the hospital where I was given an EKG. The results confirmed I had anxiety and an erratic heartbeat.

Without medication, I got worse and worse. My mother called her doctor who told her to give me Xanax. She had apprehension in giving me this pill, but it did the job and then some. For two and a half years I took the eight Xanax a day that the doctor prescribed, but I only left the house to go to the doctor.

During this time of my life, the majority of my time was spent on the sofa and in bed. My life looked the same every day. I'd wake up and take a shower. I'd go downstairs and lay on the couch. I'd watch talk shows. By afternoon I'd watch "Beaches." I memorized that movie word for word. When I'd start feeling tired, I'd go to bed. Sometimes I'd go just to sit and relax until I finally fell asleep.

I had a strong fear of getting sick, so I avoided eating and drinking any type of dairy product. I was afraid it would curdle in my stomach. My diet consisted of dry toast, crackers, and tea with sugar. I'd eat chicken noodle soup once in a while and when I felt I needed a drink other than tea I'd have water. I lost an excessive amount of weight.

The thought of leaving my house was unbearable. I'd have other people go to the store for me or do things I needed done so I wouldn't have to go out. The furthest I'd go was outside on my porch.

I was supposed to be in school. I'd try to go, but could only stay for about an hour. I worked out a deal so that I'd only have to go until 11 a.m. This worked for awhile because that is when I usually felt sick. But as my attacks worsened, I couldn't sit in a classroom at all. The last thing I wanted to do was disappoint my mother, so I'd make it look as if I was going to school. I'd sit outside all day on the front steps, rain or shine, skipping my classes. After a year of creating every excuse in the book for my poor grades, I lost hope and told my mother I was quitting school. She was upset but she knew that I wouldn't go.

After about a month, I wanted to return almost as much as my mother wanted me to. So I got into a program at my school called "Alliance." This consisted of smaller classes and group sessions. There were about 25 people in the alliance and we were like a family. I did well in all of my classes at first, but toward the end of the year I started sleeping again; sometimes because of anxiety and other times just for the hell of it, I think. I got kicked out.

I tried going back to school the next year, but the same anxiety made it impossible to go in the classrooms. I tried and tried but I just couldn't.

Through all this, I had a boyfriend. He was very understanding, but when he didn't see a change after two years, we broke up. That's when I started to do better, though. I think that's because I only had to take care of myself then. I went off medication and stopped seeing my therapist. I did well for awhile, but soon fell back once again. So I tried yet another therapist who put me on Zoloft and Klonopin.

My mother became exhausted with me. She'd tried everything she knew to help me; doctors, medications, therapy, and all the understanding she could give. She knew nothing more she could do for me.

By this time I had one friend left because of my sickness and I was determined not to lose her, too, So I made a choice, a choice to get my life back. After six months of the Klonopin, Zoloft, and new therapist, I felt no change, so I stopped these medications. My therapist disapproved, but I figured it mattered what I thought and that was that I could fight this thing with the help of my family and my friend, Laurie. I started feeling better without the medication, so I stopped seeing my therapist, too. The only counseling I needed was my family and friend. They knew me best.

I've been getting my life back together and have made new and old friends. I've been off medication for a year now. I held a seasonal job and got my driver's license. I'm doing a lot more than a year and a half ago and am feeling healthier both mentally and physically.

I'm 18 years old now. Everyday is a struggle, but it's getting easier. I've come to believe you have to learn to crawl before you can walk, and you have to learn to walk before you can run. Soon, I believe, I'll be running with the best of them again.

Susan's discomfort with enclosed spaces caused quite a stir when she shopped for clothing.

Baby Steps Out of the Ashes
by Anita L. Pace

Seventeen years ago, I sat low in the passenger seat of the car as Erin drove me to the Emergency Room of the closest hospital. Hyperventilating for nine hours by that time, I'd called the psychologist heading my support group. He told me to get to the hospital and tell the doctor I needed Valium. "It's just anxiety," he said. His words rang in my head, "Just anxiety." How could what I was feeling just be anxiety? I'd been able to drive until just a few weeks before. Suddenly, I couldn't drive and it took all I had to get out of my apartment.

My thumbs plugged my ears. Any outdoor sounds would only cause more panic. I put my legs on the dashboard. Maybe that felt like a barrier from the outside world. Index fingers from each hand laid beneath my nostrils for proof I was breathing. I had no idea how I could feel as I did and not be dying. Yet why was I surprised? I'd gone through similar, although not as lengthy, bouts for twelve years.

I'd been a shy, nervous little girl, the youngest of three children in an American-Italian-Catholic household. We lived in Inglewood, California and I thought I was very lucky. Through the eyes of a child I lived in the "greatest" state in the "greatest" country and was born into the "true" religion.

There were also things I didn't feel lucky about, like how my parents fought a lot and how there weren't a lot of kids for me to play with on my street. There were kids, but they were mostly the ages of my brother, Frank, and my sister, Geri. I loved playing baseball and became a big Dodger fan, listening to every game. I loved riding my bike, playing with my hula hoop and pogo stick, playing Parcheesi and jacks, cowboys and Indians and cops and robbers. Sometimes my brother and our neighbor Pete would have "Saturday night fights" on the front lawn, just like on TV.

We didn't really fight. But I accidentally knocked out one of Pete's teeth once. I was seven and he was ten.

I also felt nervous about many things. I was invited to Margie's birthday party, but I was afraid to go. I sat in the back seat of my parents' car as they drove home from Sears, waiting for them to say it was time for me to go to the party. When they never did, I was relieved.

My parents went to the cemetery often to visit the grave of my mother's mother. We always went there on holidays. Whether Memorial Day, Labor Day, or the 4th of July, the day began with a trip to the cemetery, followed by a picnic.

My grandmother was buried on the second floor inside a mausoleum. That word still bothers me; "Mausoleum." It's a lonely and frightening word. Could it be anything else but that for a little child walking down halls with dead bodies in walls on either side? Every step we took, ever word uttered, echoed through the stark emptiness. The huge stained glass windows depicting religious scenes were beautiful, but they couldn't over-shadow the eeriness. Engraved plates noted who was where and when they died. It was strange to discover that people who were still alive had such walls awaiting their bodies. I couldn't imagine that someday my name would be engraved in such a place with my body in a box behind it. I told myself I might not be afraid of death anymore by the time I died. Or, I thought, I might be alive when the world comes to an end. Then I'd not die, but be assumed into Heaven as long as I was worthy of it. That was my ticket; being good. Being really good.

I'd liked the elevator to my doctor's office, although very small. It had a wrought iron gate behind a door that was fun for a kid to open and close. But the elevator in the mausoleum was much bigger and scared me. It was dark and moved slow. One time my dad pushed the wrong button, sending us to the base-ment instead of the second floor. I heard voices saying there were coffins and dead bodies down there. I didn't look. I think I froze. It's no wonder that these days, when I dare venture on an elevator, I always fear the wrong button will be pushed and I'll go to the wrong floor ... maybe even to the Twilight Zone.

On another occasion, we heard a thump. "What was that?!" I asked.

"We hit a coffin." Frank said. Big brothers often protect their little sisters, but big brothers like scaring little sisters, too. Geri walked me up the stairs after that.

My mother had cancer before I was born and then had a recurrence when I was a few years old. I heard her sickness referred to as "terminal cancer" and determined that was a very bad kind of cancer. She was in and out of hospitals and more than once she had to be in the hospital at Christmas-time. After one particular surgery, I was allowed to see her. She looked horrible. I was initially glad to see her, but as soon as I walked in, she bolted up in the bed and vomited. I ran out of the room to find a nurse while my father, brother, and sister stayed put. "She's throwing up! She's throwing up!" I yelled at the nurse. In my mind I was thinking, "She's dying! She's dying!"

She didn't die, but I think her "terminal cancer" was in the back of my mind all the time ... that and the fact that I felt I was too much trouble for her. With those fears I was usually afraid to have her out of my sight. When we'd go places, I'd often hold onto her dress. "Why do you always have to hold on to me?" she'd ask. "This one always has to hold on to her Mama," she'd tell others. Sometimes she'd sound irritated. Sometimes she'd smile. Her life was rough, but she tried to be a perfect mother.

Every month, my mother's big event was shopping at the month end sales in downtown Los Angeles. As the youngest of the children, I'd have to go with her. We'd take three buses, each one more crowded, dirty, and smelly. The exhaust nauseated me.

Always shopping at the May Company first, we'd stand in a crowd of wild women a dozen rows deep, preparing for the stampede when the brave employees opened the doors at 9:30 a.m. I'd grow tired, surrounded by excited women towering over me, pushing their bodies against me as they'd attempt to better their position. I was eye-level to clutched purses and sharp elbows, next to women who either didn't see me or didn't acknowledge my existence.

Once the doors were unleashed, it was a regular cattle call; a race to the escalators or elevators, the Herald Examiner flying in the wind, open to the page of the advertised items, women fighting for the best of what was available. My only relief was when my mother would search merchandise on large square tables that had the doors open beneath them. I'd sit and rest until we'd move to her next "herding ground."

My mother didn't drive, but she walked me the three blocks to and from kindergarten. One day after school, I waited and waited, but she never came. All the other kids were gone. Maybe the teachers were, too. The thoughts through my young mind were fast and scared. "Maybe she forgot me. Maybe she's sick. Maybe I'm too much work for her and she's leaving me." I ran home frightened. My fear heightened to panic when I found no one there. "I was abandoned," I thought. I ran back to school.

I can still see my mother's smiling face as she arrived in the back seat of Mrs. Moreno's big blue boat. "How could she be smiling?" I wondered. She was always so afraid when she didn't know where I was. She was always afraid some strange man was going to get me and cut me in little pieces and put me in a box on the porch for her to discover. She was always afraid I was going to choke on fish bones or drown at Redondo Beach. So how could she smile now? My face got tight.

She'd been shopping and didn't leave on time to pick me up. My fear turned to anger. I wouldn't talk to her. That's how I showed my anger.

In the first grade, I was chosen to be one of two girls to be the "angels" for the second graders receiving their First Communion. I couldn't understand why I was chosen out of all those girls and was petrified of making a mistake. My mother wrote about this event in my Baby Book; "What I supposed to do, Mom?" she wrote in her broken English. I was afraid of attention, afraid of making mistakes, afraid of looking stupid, and afraid of being made fun of.

I wet my pants in school. I'd been told of the dirty bathrooms and I didn't want the other kids to know I ever had to go to the bathroom. I think I tried to be above life, not ever having to do what "normal" people do like relieve myself, die, things like that.

But my valiant attempts resulted in several "accidents." My mother finally threatened to take my soaked clothes and show them to the nuns if I ever wet myself again. I don't know how I managed, but I learned to hold it, just like I learned to hold in feelings.

One day while in the second grade, I felt very sick while practicing my printing. Afraid to bring attention on myself, I tried to make my printing perfect, believing perfection could make the pain go away. But the nausea increased. I was afraid of throwing up, of being sick, and of having everyone see me do it. But I was also afraid to raise my hand and tell my nun I needed to be excused. Then everyone would know something was wrong with me. I held out, hoping and praying the nausea would go away.

It didn't. Right at my desk, the inevitable began. Too late to hide anything at this point, I raced out of class, puking all the way to the bathroom. Sister Rosemarie appeared. "Are you all right?" she asked. "Yes, Sister." I couldn't admit anything was wrong even with the ugly trail of evidence that led to only me.

By the time I left the bathroom, my contribution to the hall floor was already covered with sawdust. (What did those nuns do? Keep a supply of it in the pockets of their black robes?) I returned to my seat amid stares. At lunch, no one sat within twenty feet of me, although I felt fine. But after lunch I had an encore presentation. I didn't protest when it was arranged for me to be walked home by an eighth grader. Once home, I felt fine.

I didn't love school, but I didn't hate it, either. I liked playing at recess and after lunch and I enjoyed certain subjects like spelling, geography, and history. I didn't like staying home when school was in session. I always feared going back after being sick, fearing I'd gotten behind the other kids in learning and in my homework and wouldn't be able to catch up.

My parents arguments were never physical, but the yelling petrified me. I never knew when to expect the next one, but holidays and Sunday nights were often sure bets.

My ears were keen to the sound of any potential fight. I'm positive that this fear caused me to not want anyone to come to my house. It was embarrassing, both that they fought and how afraid I got when they fought. My world felt out of control. I couldn't let anyone see such emotion in me.

Every time I heard loud voices heralding a new "encounter," I'd cringe. If in my room, I'd pace. I'd not know what to do, but I'd feel trapped. I'd start praying "Hail Mary's" fast to try to alleviate my panic and to make God stop the fighting.

One time I decided to try something new. I was on my bed reading, home alone with my parents, when a terrible fight began. I decided that I was not going to allow myself to get so afraid. After all, I thought, these fights occurred repeatedly and nothing horrible ever happened. There'd be hollering for a long time, then there'd be silence for three days. And then they'd speak to each other again.

I did my best to keep reading my book. My mother's voice bellowed and my father's soon joined in. I read the same words over and over, recalling nothing, yet telling myself nothing bad was going to happen. My attempt at remaining calm ended abruptly with the one sentence I'll never forget out of my mother's mouth; "I'm going to kill myself!" I rushed to her as I heard the bathroom door close and lock. I felt myself losing my life and felt alone in trying to save both my mother's and, in essence, my own life. I knew she had pills in the medicine cabinet. Both of my parents took Librium and Miltown for "their nerves." I banged the door with both fists. "Mom! Mom! Open the door!!!"

It was several minutes before she came out. I was a wreck. "Did you spit them all out?!" I kept asking. She wasn't sure.

I'd used humor before to make life in my house more livable. Now I laid next to my mother in bed, a girl of 10, thinking of every possible imitation I'd developed thus far in my life to make my mother laugh. The best I could get was a weak smile. By the time I got to bed, I was exhausted. I also felt I'd learned a lesson; if I don't act panicky or like I care when I do, terrible things can happen. I didn't think my mother would have done this had I shown my panic sooner.

Despite the stories I'm recalling here, my childhood also included many good memories; the Good Humor ice cream man, the Helm's Bakery man, playing with Frank and Geri on the mostly beautiful days in Southern California, going to parks and to the beach, having two birthday parties every year, one with the adults, one with kids, going to Disneyland, and enjoying television in the days when there were only happy endings unless watching The Twilight Zone.

Life changed when my sister married. I was 11. Frank, 15, was gone more often and I felt very lonely.

At 13, with only one year left at my grammar school, my family moved to northeast Los Angeles. Our house was new, but in a hilly area. There was no grass to play on, just ivy and ice plant. There was no one to play with and it seemed my toys had disappeared. Keeping a promise, my mother let me get a dog. Tiny became my best friend. The little brown mutt was always excited to see me. She wanted nothing more than to be with me.

It was decided I'd go to the public school for the eighth grade. I didn't know what that would be like, not wearing a uniform, being one of those "public school kids" us Catholic school kids always felt better than.

Being weird was about the worst thing you could be called. Well, maybe "nerd" was worse. Either way, I felt very weird. I wore bobby socks and the other girls wore nylons. I had thick eyebrows and the other girls' brows were plucked. I had hairy legs and wasn't allowed to shave like most the other girls.

My clothes were from the bargain basement and from a different era than that of the others. I was smart without trying. I had to fight myself from standing when answering questions. Kids giggled when I did, but I'd been trained to do so. So much of what I'd been told was right was suddenly wrong. So much of what I'd been told was wrong was acceptable.

It was 1964, an election year. Democrat Lyndon Johnson faced Republican Barry Goldwater. Nice kids wore Goldwater buttons. Nice kids had Republican parents. How could this be? Republicans didn't care about people was the message I got. How could these nice kids not care about people? I was confused and wished I was back at St. Anselm's with the nuns and the kids I'd known, some since the first grade.

One day in math class, the teacher decided to pit one girl against one boy to solve math problems at the blackboard. The girls picked me. I was surprised because no one in that class had ever talked to me. I wasn't especially good at math, but I was better than the rest of them. What was average in Catholic school was brilliant in this public school. The boys picked Herb Van der Veer.

I saw all the girls looking at me. Then Miss Lappin gave us several problems to solve in front of everyone. There I tried to prove myself, standing in front of the class, a pimply-faced, old-fashioned dressed, hairy-legged girl. Herb killed me. I couldn't figure the problems as fast as he could. I felt inferior in every way and sat down, feeling I'd let down the girls and lost my chance to be accepted by them.

In retrospect, it's no surprise how I suddenly felt sick in this class days later. It was a sick I'd never felt before; nauseated, but I didn't think I was going to throw up. I was hot, so I took off my sweater. I stared at the clock. There were thirty minutes to go before the class would end, but I wanted to get out and I wanted to get out NOW. I knew I couldn't just leave. That wasn't acceptable and I could only do acceptable things. Every second was like an hour of time. I felt things I'd never felt before, frightening feelings. I'd heard of losing one's mind. This had to be what is was like. What else could it be but that or dying?

I was never so happy to hear the bell indicating the end of class as I was in that class. I rushed out and felt fine. How strange, I thought. What was it and would it happen again?

Of course it happened again and again, beginning with once a week in math classes and graduating to most every day in every class. I forced myself to stay in my seat. I couldn't bear the attention of being seen leaving a class, the possible ridicule or even the concern. Everything had to be all right. I had to be all right. I didn't want to be a bother. I didn't feel worthy of such attention.

These episodes came and went. I'd go for weeks experiencing these "things" daily and then they'd go away for awhile. I never knew when to expect them, but they only came to me while in classrooms and occasionally during Mass, too.

After I graduated from high school, my family moved again. This time it was just myself and my parents because Frank got married. I got a summer job at a cafeteria. There I made my first close friend in my life. I was drawn to her immediately and so was she to me. Jackie was fun and did everything I didn't do. She smoked, she drank, and had a boyfriend. She wasn't afraid to go against the status quo. That scared me and intrigued me at the same time. I liked some breaking of rules for once. I fell in love with her but didn't know what to call it because I certainly wasn't "one of those." I spent whatever time I could with her at work, at her parents' house, and at a coffee shop where we drank tea and talked.

When summer was over, I quit this job and began college. I didn't know what career to pursue, so college gave me something to do. I majored in Foreign Language. It sounded better than anything else I thought capable of. Journalism, Theater Arts, and Broadcasting appealed to me, but I thought I could never have a performance type career. And they weren't practical. My mother thought I should be a teacher, but I hated school. My father thought I'd be secure in Civil Service, but he was miserable in Civil Service. I was concerned about studying something that would lead to a job. I read the help wanted ads every day to see what looked interesting. Nothing looked interesting!

Every morning while in the bathroom I felt awful. It wasn't physical and yet it was. I'd have a feeling of dread, that all was horrible and always would be. I'd feel I was going to go crazy from this feeling, but then it would pass.

Then in college, the sharp pains in my gut began on cue at 8 a.m. when Italian 1 began. I liked Professor Abondolo, but my stomach must not have. I'd stay in my seat and sweat it out until the pains subsided. I soon discovered Pepto Bismol and started carrying the bottle of the pink stuff in my purse. When the pain would appear, I'd pull it out and take a swig. I quit school and spent hours every day sitting in a chair in the backyard, feeling unable to do much of anything but think of Jackie.

On February 9, 1971 a powerful earthquake hit Los Angeles. My parents panicked but I remained in bed until they forced me under the dining room table. I wasn't afraid until I saw how petrified they were.

I forced myself to apply for a job at the new NBC commissary and got it. I was very scared at first, afraid of making mistakes, but in a short time I began to feel better. I liked making money, being useful, and I liked the environment.

Other than that, time spent with Jackie was about all I cared about. We spoke about getting our own place together someday. Up until that time, I thought I'd end up living with my parents the rest of my life because I knew I never wanted to get married, and getting married was the only acceptable way out of my house. Freedom was something I'd always wanted, but hadn't realized it, maybe because it seemed impossible.

One night I conjured up all my courage and told my parents I was going to move out in a month. I was 19, but my mother got hysterical. "I should have known this would happen!" she cried. "You made me laugh last night. Tonight you make me cry!" She was very superstitious and uncomfortable with happiness. I learned to do the same.

My father's response was to tell me that if I can tell them when I'm leaving, they can tell me to leave. And so he told me to leave that night. As I packed some things, he called my brother to ask if I could stay with him and my sister-in-law, Sharon. For the first time in my life, I felt free. The anxiety I felt every morning in the bathroom disappeared. But then a new set of problems entered my life. I had to pay bills and deal with the real world which I'd never known before.

Three weeks later, on St. Patrick's Day of 1971, Jackie and I got an apartment. I worked 40 hours during the day and took up to four classes at night. I felt less of those feelings in night classes than in those during the day. I ate all I could at work as I didn't have much money for dinner or anything else.

I went through a roller coaster ride with Jackie. We had some great times but we had some horrible times, too. After eight months of living together, she got married. I felt devastated. I moved in with an aunt for two months and after feeling stronger, got my own apartment. It was during this time that I went to my first therapist. I got to talk to Liz and tell her anything and everything and she never showed any judgment with what I said. When she left L.A. for San Francisco, I was very sad, but she'd given me a taste of something I'd never known before.

After five years at a two year college, I received an AA degree. It was 1974. That year that I discovered that I was "one of those," even if I didn't hate men or want to drive a truck (as I thought "one of thoses" were like.) I felt a peace I'd never known before. I changed my major to sociology and transferred to the university to get my BA.

The university intimidated me. It was big and had many buildings, full classes and packed parking lots. I was determined to do well and sat with two women I befriended. One was in her forties and took nonstop notes. I wondered what she was writing and I felt afraid that I couldn't keep up with her.

It wasn't long after that that the same old feelings hit again, and they hit hard. Every time they'd gone away, they'd come back with a variation in symptoms, like a mutation of a virus. I had classes straight through from 8 a.m. until 1 p.m. and I'd go through the sensations in every class; feeling I couldn't breathe, feeling I wasn't real, feeling I had to get out or I'd lose my mind. I jerked in my seat, crossing my legs repeatedly. I took sudden, unexpected gasps of air. I feared people would notice how strange I behaved. Among the classes I took was Abnormal Psychology. There was a small section of one page dedicated to a topic called "Agoraphobia." It looked like an awful thing to have and I was glad I didn't have it. Little did I know. In time, the feelings came on while driving to the university. I decided to see a counselor on campus.

Doris was great. She told me I was having anxiety attacks and we talked about my life. As Liz had done, Doris listened to me. It made me want to become a therapist.

By this time I was in my first relationship. There'd been a quick courtship followed by a quicker commitment. At long last somebody wanted me and so I jumped for it, believing no one was likely to ever want a low creature like me again. But initial adoration was not to be believed. Her apparent love turned sour quickly. This first relationship ended only after one and a half years.

Friends introduced me to Erin. A friendship grew into a romantic relationship within months. Erin was much more loving than my first partner, but problems again appeared. I wondered why I had so much difficulty in sustaining a good relationship. I wondered what I lacked and I figured I must be the problem.

All this time I worked in social work settings as part of my training; first with the mentally handicapped and then at a clinic for troubled kids.

When I graduated from college in 1976, I was elated. I recall the group of 30 at the restaurant after the ceremony. An expensive meal was before me, but I couldn't eat it. I couldn't sit down and I couldn't swallow.

I continued working at the clinic for a year, but I quit because the male receptionist worked half the hours I did, yet made twice the amount of money. I hadn't heard the word "assertive" as yet.

Out of work for several weeks, I felt increasingly anxious about leaving the house and looking for another job. I'd go out but feel dizzy and have trouble breathing. I'd feel I had to race home. It was much like craving a cold drink on a hot day. I had to get home and nothing was fast enough.

I got a job in a cafeteria again. I'd swore after college that I'd never work around food again and was disappointed in myself. I felt like a failure, but there was no way I could even get through a job interview for a "real" job and I had bills to pay. Performing a social work job seemed impossible, but running around like a maniac waiting on customers allowed me to rid myself of some sensations. College could offer the opportunity to earn a degree, but it couldn't make me capable of dealing with emotionally troubled people, including myself. My life consisted of working, eating, watching a little TV at night, going to bed, and doing it all over again the next day.

Erin called me at work one day. "There's people on AM Los Angeles talking about something that sounds like what you have," she said. People were talking about having trouble being in crowds, eating in restaurants, traveling, going to the movies, riding elevators, and being alone . The problem was called Agoraphobia and the self help group on TV was called TERRAP. I got an appointment and was relieved when the psychologist diagnosed me as "moderately Agoraphobic." I actually had something that had a name and I wasn't the only one who had it.

Erin accompanied me to the meetings. There were about 15 phobics with support persons. I sat and compared my abilities to others. "I can't even drive one block," a woman in her 50's said. "Who can't even drive one block?" I thought. With all my limitations, I thought this woman weak.

It was December of 1977. I'd lived in the same apartment for six years. One man and several women moved in next door. They were noisy and often up all night. Already fatigued, I'd be awakened by banging on the walls in the middle of the night. One time I heard screaming and one of the women ran from the apartment. I told the owner and he went to talk to them.

Nothing changed. In fact, the noise got worse and other tenants became intimidated by this tenant. I'd begun practicing assertiveness in my life, but hadn't yet learned there are times it's assertive to decide to do nothing. So when I was awakened four times one night, I decided to take matters into my own hands.

Half asleep, I banged on the neighbor's door. A quick exchange of verbal blows led to Vince grabbing my arm three different times. Determined to show I meant business, I dared him to do it again. This well-built ex GI complied and told me to go back into my apartment. Thinking I couldn't let him get away with this, I slugged him in the chest, seeing rage in his eyes as my fist made contact. Moments later, I saw his right fist begin to raise. The next thing I recall was my head feeling like a pancake. I lied on the ground, curled in the corner near my apartment door. Someone was on top of me, slugging me in the back. "I'm going to be beaten to a pulp," I thought. I thought it strange to think of a cliché at a time like that. "I'm going to die." I heard Erin screaming for Byron, another neighbor, to help. Vince hit Erin while a woman slugged away at me.

"Get back into your apartment, Vince." I heard Byron say. Byron had a stutter, but he didn't stutter now. "I'm calling the police." And then I felt a body get off of mine. The thought occurred that I wasn't going to die after all. Byron Furgol may have saved my life that night.

When I was resigned to death, I had no fear or pain. But once I realized I was going to live, I felt a fear I'd never known. I reached for my door handle from my knees, not wanting to take the time to stand up. I scurried into my apartment, dead bolting it behind me. I didn't want to open it again.

When the police arrived, I shook so severely that I had to clamp my jaw to form words. "Off the record," one officer said, "I wouldn't press charges. He'll be out in a few hours." The thought of Vince's anger of being taken to jail because of me was more than I could fathom. I didn't press charges.

The nurse in the ER couldn't have looked less concerned if she'd been overdosed on Valium. It was 4 a.m. by the time we got to bed at Rick and Gary's, but I was at work at 8 a.m. I didn't think I had reason to call in sick. The x ray showed a slightly broken nose .

For three weeks, Erin and I lived from friend to friend. Then we moved into an apartment that felt safe. For several weeks I continued going to the self help group, but I spent most of the time in the lounge, hyperventilating on the sofa. Not until each group session ended was I able to go in the room and be comfortable. I believed everyone else was going to get better but myself. I'd be ill forever.

I took home the written materials and learned about relaxation, desensitization, assertiveness, feelings, and baby steps. The psychologist once asked me "How do you feel?"

"I feel like the agitation cycle of the washing machine," I said.

"That's not a feeling," he said. But that's all I could identify as a feeling. We made goals and listed steps to these goals. A goal could be as simple as getting out the door. No matter what the goal, there were steps to break them down into. This was difficult for me. I'd always been impatient.

Despite severe anxiety, I'd always been able to work. One day, about five months after the assault, I looked up from the cash register. A man, similar-looking to Vince, stood before me. My body bolted backwards as if hit all over again. Within days, I had a major panic attack at work. I ran out of the store and walked frantically around the neighborhood.

The same thing happened again the next day and I knew I couldn't function. Feeling I surrendered to this thing, I walked off the job and to the personnel office. "I need to go on disability," I said. I couldn't fight it anymore, at least not at work. I was burned out, exhausted.

At 26, I had nothing to look forward to. I had no energy. I enjoyed nothing. I couldn't work. I couldn't have fun. I couldn't play or eat without panic. Empathy appeared quickly for the woman who'd said she couldn't even drive one block. I'd become virtually housebound, leaving my apartment only to go to the meetings and getting the mail down the stairs.

I'd awaken in the same clothes that I'd fall asleep in. Why change? I wasn't going anywhere. I didn't have the energy to do so anyway. My days were spent hyperventilating, panicking, and trying to concentrate on the soap operas from the sofa. I attempted to swallow food, but choked often, even when nothing was in my mouth. There was a heaviness in my head and I felt as if there was a band of steel tightened around it. My chest was so tight. I felt for my pulse all day to prove myself still alive, whoever I now was. Who I'd been became a memory. Who I'd become was a nightmare.

My only relief was in the few hours I slept at night, but sleeping wasn't without its torment. I'd pace the bedroom floor until 2 a.m. when I'd finally collapse from fatigue. But most nights I'd awaken in a panic several times, bolting up in bed and gasping for air as if I'd not breathed for several minutes.

I'd been afraid of pills, afraid of them making me feel more strange and out of control than I already felt. I feared, too, having an anaphylactic reaction. The thought of dying from my throat closing was more than I could bear, despite all the hours I'd already felt I wasn't breathing.

I'd experience hours of hyperventilation and panic many times, but the nine hours this time was all the anguish I could take. On the way to the Emergency Room, I concentrated on the relief Valium would give me, if only for a little while.

The doctor told Erin to leave the room. Then he sat and spoke with me. He prescribed 30 milligrams of Valium a day. He also suggested I dress more feminine and visit him at the hospital. Despite my state of mind, I knew this doctor was out of line, but I just nodded to everything he said. I wanted the damn Valium. I wanted relief far more than I wanted to discuss ethics with this doctor, far more than I feared possible side effects of the drug. I went home a little more relaxed and decided to only take the pills when I absolutely needed them. I didn't want to pop a pill every time I got anxious. I'd be taking pills all day.

It was the night before my 27th birthday when I awakened with a new sensation. I felt like ... nothingness. Like an empty shell. I jumped out of bed to prove I was alive, but I thought my body and soul had separated. How many more symptoms could I experience?

The night I'd gone to the hospital, my psychologist had said, "It's just anxiety." I couldn't get his words out of my mind. "Just anxiety." What did that mean? That it couldn't kill me? If this is anxiety, what's it like to really be sick? It was 1978 and I'd already suffered since 1965. But the huge realization I had was that specialists couldn't cure me. People who knew all about panic disorder and agoraphobia couldn't cure me. There was no magic cure. *I* was going to have to make myself better. *Me*. Weak, scared, inadequate *me*. *I* had to do the work to improve. *I* had to take the steps, the baby steps, that I felt so impatient with. *My future was in my hands.*

Panic attacks began at 2 p.m. every afternoon and continued for about 12 hours every day. I felt exhausted and panicked several hours every day, but I had to somehow make changes. Sitting up felt impossible, but I made myself get up for a minute or so at a time during commercials. I forced myself into the kitchen to wash dishes and make dinner this way. I had to fight the urge to lie down, but I'd tell myself, "It's just for a minute and then I can lie down again."

As much as a waste as it seemed, I made myself change my clothes every day. I no longer allowed myself to go to bed in the same clothes I was in all day. I'd not spend 24 hours, seven days a week, wearing the same stinking clothes.

My neighbor beneath me asked if I'd start letting her dog, Buddy, out on her patio every day after the mail carrier came. This was a commitment that seemed monumental. It involved going out my front door, going down the stairs, going into her apartment, and then letting Buddy out before returning to my refuge. My apartment wasn't all that "safe," but while in there I wasn't outside for the world to see me falling apart. I agreed to do it.

I knew nutrition was important. I knew stress burned up vitamins. I knew the black circles under my eyes and lost weight were indicators of my failed health. I had to eat more and had to eat nutritious food. I knew I was less likely to choke on non-fibrous foods.

I forced myself to the Westward Ho Market down the street. Although that in itself rushed me past many baby steps, I bought Malt-O-Meal and wheat germ for breakfast. I bought several jars of baby food, mostly vegetables. Squash, sweet potatoes (my favorite), carrots and custard went into my cart. I was petrified of the checkout line, feeling trapped. I swayed, feeling an inner earthquake of giant proportions able to knock me over, so I pretended to tie my shoes so I could stay close to the ground. No one seemed to notice I was wearing thongs.

I panicked all the way to the health food store, but I found a vitamin-mineral-amino acid powder suggested by an employee. It tasted awful, but adding sugar and refrigeration helped enough for me to drink it. I pictured it replenishing depleted cells throughout my body.

When I'd been approved for Social Security Disability, I initially thought all my problems were over. I'd get financial help and never again have to do work I hated. Brought up strictly, the thought having no responsibilities sounded like a relief. It was and it wasn't. Never having had to make my own schedule, I felt lost with planning my days. Instead of being relaxing, it was a responsibility to have no responsibilities. It was a burden. I needed some responsibilities to have meaning. I needed to bring some discipline back into my life. I'd figured I'd be on disability for six months initially, but hadn't realized I was falling apart and had to fall apart completely before being able to begin building myself once again.

I found a program on TV called Yoga for Health. I hated slow exercises. I hated exercising. But I made myself stretch while watching this program five days a week. I got better at some things, but never got much limber at others. It was okay. I wasn't on the sofa. I was doing something. And I was more disciplined.

I made myself go outside, although very anxious. I attempted to use TERRAP'S desensitization program where one goes into a stressful situation and retreats when beyond a "3" in anxiety and then approaches it again. I was at "7" through "10's" most days all day, so this plan didn't work well for me. I made myself walk up and down the street. I just prayed no one would try to talk to me. I'd feel pulled to the right side, like a power dragging me off the sidewalk. I practiced driving. Around the block I'd go, over and over and over, slowly expanding my perimeters. I accepted that I wasn't going to suddenly be able to drive anywhere I wanted. As I drove further, I did the seemingly impossible, giving myself permission to pull to the side of the road if I became too anxious. I learned that giving myself this freedom was more important than driving somewhere in a panic.

My life became one big self help program. Everything I did was a job, although most people wouldn't understand the elation of walking down the street with little stress. I practiced relaxation exercises with tapes I had, even though I often panicked right as I'd think I'd relaxed.

My social life consisted of people in my apartment building and people I met through TERRAP. Get-togethers were possible because we all understood the limitations of the others.

One particular New Year's Day a few of us got together. There was a minor earthquake and all the spouse's support people panicked. We agoraphobics were calm as could be. Maybe we only panic in light of no danger. I began working the Jumble Puzzle in the paper every day to stimulate my mind, or at least a different one than I stimulated with panic. I bought mugs and learned to decorate them with sayings like, "Relax." I stopped watching the news and cut out all daytime TV. It was sad that

Luke and Laura's life on General Hospital had come to mean more to me than my own.

I began baking cookies for the coffee shop of a therapist I saw. First I delivered them to her house. After several months, I began delivering them 13 miles away.

I went to the supermarket with no shopping in mind. What I took was a notebook and pen. I'd realized I often was anxious in markets because I was confused. So I marked which items were in which aisles. I'd not get the anxiety of looking for the cereal or parmesan cheese or anything else this way.

I enrolled in an assertiveness training class. I'd never been able to complain about a product, return a product, get off the phone when I wanted to, tell anyone if I disagreed with them. I began learning how to, although I knew it would take years of practice and the decision to speak up in a way I was not comfortable with or used to.

I needed money and took a job calling from my home for the City of Hope. Speaking on the phone was difficult for me. Always feeling pressure on my chest, I knew I sounded strange because of how I breathed. I got $1.25 every time a person agreed to collect money from their neighborhood for that organization. I made about $15 a week during this temporary job.

Although receiving a Disability check, it was not enough to live on. During the Reagan administration, the definition of "disability" was modified. Twice during his reign, I was cut from Social Security. "According to Social Security regulations, you are no longer considered disabled." I kept reading the words. I could barely speak on the phone. It was an event to go to the grocery store. Everything I did involved severe anxiety and dealing with it best I could. And I had a letter that said I was able to go back to working in a cafeteria. Whomever made that determination never worked in a cafeteria and knew nothing about me. Thousands of people were cut off the rolls, some with heart disease and cancer. I read in the newspaper how several people died after being terminated. And some committed suicide.

Besides the financial impact of being cut off, this meant I was no longer entitled to food stamps. I had to apply for work at the employment office. The system was crazier than me.

I had to hire attorneys for the two occasions to appeal my case. It took four months for the hearings and another four months for the payments to be reinstated. Each time, the attorneys got 25% of the back payments.

During those months, I had to rely on a credit card and the person I was living with. Erin was helpful, but the strain of my dependence proved fatal to our relationship. I recognized that when I got better, I'd also be single. But she didn't want to abandon me when most debilitated.

Not all therapists were helpful. Two come to mind. They were interns for a program for homebound patients and came to my apartment. I was initially grateful, but Phyllis had a way about her. "You must be very comfortable not having to go outside and have any responsibility," she said in her New York accent. Just what I needed. More guilt. Or was she trying to make me feel angry, thinking that would help. She had absolutely no idea what it took for me to accomplish anything in the course of a day. I was weak, but not dead. I wrote them a strong letter and told them to not return. "What's this bullshit?" was the response to my letter. I guess what they said to me was all right. But my saying I didn't like it, wasn't.

I "came out" to people about having agoraphobia and panic disorder. It was relieving, but it was also painful for me when people who I thought understood my limitations vocalized their discontent. The more I got out, the more some people thought that meant I wasn't going through Hell when I often was.

"I resent it," one said, "that I have to work and part of my money goes to pay you." It was my pride that kept me from bursting into tears. I thought she understood. "Do you want to trade with me?" I should have asked. "Here, you get in my shoes and feel like you're going to choke every time you eat, and I'll live your life. Here, you deal with what I feel when I get on the phone, when I leave my apartment, when I go to the grocery store, when I attempt to be with my family during the holidays. You stand in my shoes and I will do your job without fearing or experiencing panic."

There were many times I hurt the feelings of well-meaning people. "You wouldn't feel anxiety in the elevator with me, would you?" some asked. "You wouldn't feel anxious in the restaurant with me, would you?" "You wouldn't panic if I came to visit you, would you?" "You'd be okay in the car if I was with you, wouldn't you?" They had no idea. They couldn't stop me from feeling trapped, couldn't stop me from choking. Why would I feel more comfortable with the thought of embarrassing myself in front of someone who knew me? Yes, there was a fear of being alone, but that didn't mean I felt safe with others. How would their being in the elevator keep me safe? If it got stuck, we'd both be trapped. They meant well. How could I make them understand something I was just grasping the meaning of?

"How long are you going to have this?" was a less compassionate question asked. "I think your therapist is taking you for a ride. I heard that most people get over this. I think you just don't want to do things you don't want to do. Everyone gets anxious, but we have to do things anyway." These sentences came from a relative.

I started therapy through the County. I was anxious talking in a small room, sharing my thoughts the best that I could. I didn't know it when I began, but I'd spend four and a half years with Shirley, going through many experiences, learning a lot about myself and about life. At first I had to push to drive the four miles to her office. In time, she moved and I pushed and succeeded in driving 11 miles to see her.

Therapy was one hour a week. I had many hours to fill and I looked for ways to make me grow and participate more in life, even if limited. I'd always hated puzzles, but I bought one with 2000 pieces. It would make me think and concentrate. It was something to complete ... which I did. I pulled two old dressers out on my balcony and refinished them. Without knowing how, I made a bookcase. I wrote affirmations, over and over and over again. "I am lovable. I am capable. I am worthy. I am intelligent. I am sensitive. I deserve happiness." I listened to subliminal tapes. What did I have to lose? I rode my bicycle around the neighborhood everyday.

Did I feel better? Yes and no. I had anxiety most of the time, but I had more semblance of a life as I did more. I was doing something besides lying around, getting weaker and weaker and hyperventilating. I felt somewhat better doing things rather than lying there, taking my pulse. I learned to divert my attention. I couldn't continue concentrating on every breath I took.

I came into contact with a woman who did Neo-Reichian work. I would drive several miles to Meri's house, then talk, beat pillows, cry, scream, and basically do what I'd not allowed anyone to ever see me do, including myself. Then I'd clean her house in return.

My new activities taught me things. Selling cookies, I learned about bulk prices. I got a business name, figured my cost per cookie, and did paperwork. Delivering cookies meant getting out of the apartment, having a destination, getting some money for what I did, and having the satisfaction of making something with my hands.

One major help to myself was writing a journal. At first I didn't know what to write. "Walked one block to Baskin-Robbins," one of my first entries read. Within months I wrote several pages a day. On therapy days, I'd recall most of what my therapist and I said and write it all down. That journal became a friend I looked forward to spending time with every day. I noticed, too, that my concentration improved, as well as my memory.

I did volunteer work at a local cable television company. Although a big step, I learned how to run a camera and do various tasks in a studio. The variety and freedom of motion helped me deal with any anxiety I felt.

In the mid 80's, I took a screen writing course. I made myself comfortable by sitting in the back of the room. I took other writing classes, and compiled several rejection letters from magazines, but a few of my articles were printed in the Sunday paper. A story about having agoraphobia was published in an anthology of women with disabilities, "With the Power of Each Breath."

I took part-time jobs, mostly working for neighbors. Then I got work cleaning houses. I did this for almost three years. It was during this time that a new old stress entered my life.

In 1987, after a year and a half battle, my mother died of cancer. It was a terrible time, but I kept putting one foot in front of the other. After she died, I joined a basketball class, one of two women with men. I'd been emotionally exhausted. I figured my physical exhaustion would do me good and it did.

When I was 39, I moved from Los Angeles to Oregon. I'd long known that the city had become too big, too out of control for me to live in. I'd begun fearing my obituary. What if I got cancer like my mother did at a young age? How many years did I have left? What would be said about me after my death? "She had so much potential?" "She was funny, but so alone?" With those fears in mind, I pretended to have the courage to move away from the area I'd always known. I awakened with gasps of panic again after years of reprieve, but I didn't let the gasps stop me. I had to move. I had to take more chances. I had to push beyond what I'd ever pushed before. I fear my mortality. I fear dying before making a mark on this world. Perhaps dying without having lived has been my greatest fear and maybe that fear has been the driving force behind each baby step that I've taken.

What has caused my anxiety? Was it a strict upbringing with fear of God and guilt over every thought and deed, or was it simply the gene pool I drew from? I don't know. I do know that I've spent years trying to help myself using a variety of techniques: speaking to therapists about my past and present, utilizing biofeedback, practicing relaxation techniques, writing positive affirmations, and taking vitamins, minerals, amino acids and herbs to be physically healthier. I've also had chiropractic adjustments and acupuncture treatments. Maybe several of these "therapies" helped me, maybe not. I've even prayed for a cure, but I learned early on that churches seemed to bring on anxiety attacks.

I'd wanted to get well without medications, partly because I feared their side effects and dependency. But after years of much work and minimal improvement, I resorted to this option. I tried a few antidepressant, but although they work well for many, I had trouble tolerating them. Through trial and error, I found I best responded to Klonopin and an occasional Xanax. I was surprised when I felt a sense of normalcy I'd not felt since preteen days.

My growth continues, not without the aid of a medication, not without difficulty in certain situations. But I've managed to publish three books now, an accomplishment I'd have thought impossible several years ago.

I see a psychologist who utilizes a therapy called Eye Movement Desensitization and Reprocessing (EMDR). It's been especially helpful for people with post traumatic stress and has been beneficial for many with panic disorder and phobias. It's too early for me to say how much it's helping me, but I figure it's worth a try.

My life today is so much better than when I was 26 and feared I'd spend the rest of my life hyperventilating on my sofa. It's been 30 years since my first panic attack in that eighth grade class. Had I known beforehand that thousands of hours of terror would rip away most of my teens, twenties, and a portion of my thirties, the depression would've been devastating. I've known anxiety most of my life, but with all I've experienced, I am alive and glad to have come as far as I have, to live in a time when there is a name for what I have as well as treatment, even if not perfect.

There was a time I was too anxious to even speak on the phone. Yet tomorrow I board a jet to attend the funeral of a young man my age, nearly to the day, taken by a brain tumor. I'm afraid to fly, but I trust I'll deal with it. Ronald's illness and death shocked anyone who knew him. As well as being a good man, father, husband, brother, friend and employer, he lived life fully. He wasn't afraid of flying in any sense of the word. It's a lesson for me and everyone else to live as happily and fully as we can. And while a grievous experience, attending the services will allow me to participate in a reality of life. And isn't that what recovery is? It's not being without problems, pain, or sadness. It's being able to play whatever hand you are dealt every day.

I realized that I am stronger than I thought, and I've learned much from the challenges I've faced; about getting healthier in my own way and time, about compassion for myself and others, about allowing myself to not be perfect (as if I ever could be) and about the importance of loving and accepting myself as I am. My life isn't without setbacks or doubts at times and the challenges continue. But I no longer feel unworthy of love or happiness. I no longer just try to survive. From out of the ashes, these baby steps found a life.

What is Cognitive-Behavioral Therapy?

Cognitive-behavioral therapy (CBT) teaches patients to anticipate the situations and bodily sensations that are associated with their panic attacks. This awareness sets the stage for helping the patient to control the attacks. Specially trained therapists tailor CBT to the specific needs of each patient. The therapy usually includes the following components:

° Helping identify and change patterns of thinking that cause patients to misperceive commonplace events or situations as dangerous and then "thinking the worst." Patients are often unaware of how deeply these anxiety-provoking thoughts are ingrained.

° Teaching patients exercises to prevent the hyperventilation that often triggers a panic attack. The exercises help the patient to replace alarmist thoughts as "I'm dying" with more appropriate ones as "I'm just hyperventilating. I can handle this."

° Helping patients become less fearful by safely and gradually exposing them to situations and physical sensations they avoid or find frightening.

CBT is a short-term treatment, typically lasting 12-15 sessions over several months. Patients with panic disorder who go through CBT are reported to have very few adverse effects.

Information provided by the National Institute of Mental Health pamphlet "Panic Disorder Treatment and Referral"

The Quest for the Perfect Tree
by Susan Turner

She used to say to me
    look at that magnificent tree ... or
    look at those blossoming flowers
on our treacherous weekly walks.

I knew her manipulations ...
what she was trying to have me do
    but I was far smarter than she knew...
My eyes stayed planted on the street
    glaring at the asphalt beneath my feet.

I was never into nature anyway.
Trees, flowers, skies, mountains were just a part
    of the world
    that was to be rushed past
except for the menacing dry brown mountain
    that I can see out my front window.

Each summer as the heat rises and the hot winds
    whip up
I wait apprehensively for it to erupt
into vivid flames of red and orange
    as it did thirty years ago.

Last winter I saw the sky
    especially before and after storms.
The startling blackness of the clouds, with the
silver moon or radiant sun
    attempting to break through
    embodied me.

For years the stormy darkness frightened me
      with threats of booming thunder and
      brilliant lightning.
Last winter I rushed out to catch the dramatic
sky
      fear was forgotten.

The sky became a centering force
      a vast expanse to focus my attention on
      when there was a need within me.
I wondered if the winter sky had always been
      so beautiful.

Last summer I saw the ocean
      in its peaceful beauty and turbulent
      moods.
As each wave washed to the sand
      my mind was cleansed and
      the grip I held so tightly on my body
      lessened.

For years the ocean was just a thing to lay near
      as I scorched my skin,
      dying for that golden tan.

Last summer my chilling childhood memories
of horrendous waves
      crashing into my tiny body
      enveloping me in black coldness
and the taste of putrid salt water in my mouth
left me.

In the sea's serenity
      I found my own ... if only fleeting.
I wondered if the ocean had always been so
healing.

Last fall I saw the trees
    with their leaves pulsing vibrant hues
    of red, orange, and golden yellow.
For years these trees stirred an uneasiness within
    me
    as gutsy winds caused them to sway and
    bend.

Last fall I went on a quest for the perfect tree.
I parked my car on foreign streets and stopped
traffic
    to capture an autumn tree's beauty
    before its fiery leaves fell to the waiting
curb.
I was risking my "safety" as I ventured through
    unfamiliar territories.

My quest for the perfect tree took the focus off of
    me.
I wondered if the fall trees had always been so
magnificent.

If she and I were still to take our weekly walks
I would be drawing *her* attention to all of nature's
    wonders.
I would not be using nature
    as she once tried to have me do.

I am now in harmony with the trees
    skies   clouds   mountains
    and flowers.
And I would want to share my awakening with
    her.

My eyes would never even notice
    the gravely asphalt beneath my feet.

    (And I would probably trip.)

Where can I get more information about Panic Disorder and Agoraphobia?

The National Institute for Mental Health Resource list provides information, including scientific articles and books, general consumer books and pamphlets, self-help information, and videotapes.

For a copy of the list, call 1-800-64-PANIC.

Other Resources of Information:

National Institute for Mental Health
Panic Campaign
Room 15C-05
5600 Fishers Lane
Rockville, MD 20857
(301) 443-4513

National Alliance for the Mentally Ill (NAMI)
200 N. Glebe Road., Suite 1015
Arlington, VA 22203-3754
(703) 524-7600
FAX (703) 524-9094
Email:NAMIofc@AOL.com

Anxiety Disorders Association of America
(ADAA)
6000 Executive Blvd., Suite 200
Rockville, MD 20852
(301) 231-9350

American Psychiatric Association
1400 K Street, N.W.
Washington, D.C. 20005
(202) 682-6000

American Psychological Association
750 First Street, N.E.
Washington, D.C. 20002
(202) 336-5500

Newsletters

The Panic Relief News
981 Shepard Avenue
North Brunswick, NJ 08902-2252

NPAD News
(National Panic and Anxiety Newsletter)
Cyma J. Siegel, Editor
1718 Burgandy Place, Suite B
Santa Rosa, CA 95403

On Target
(Newsletter of Freedom from Fear)
Mary Guardino
308 Seaview Avenue
Staten Island, NY 10305

Straight Talk
Joan Orrico, Editor
1006 Huguenot Ave.
Staten Island, NY 10312

ENcourage Newsletter
Pat Merrill, Editor
13610 N. Scottsdale Road, Suite 10-126
Scottsdale, AZ 85254

ABIL Newsletter
(Agoraphobics Building Independent Lives)
Shirley Green
1418 Lorraine Avenue
Richmond, VA 23227

The P.A.N.I.C. Press NEWSLETTER
Charles R. Cobb, M.D.
2642 E. 21st Street
Tulsa, OK 74114-1740

Less Stress Press
Midwest Center
106 N. Church Street Suite 200
Oak Harbor, OH 43449

PM NEWS
Anxiety and Phobia Clinic
White Plains Hospital Center
Davis Avenue and East Post Road
White Plains, NY 10601

The Open Door Newsletter
608 Russell Avenue South
Minneapolis, MN 55405

ADAA Reporter
(Anxiety Disorder Assoc. of America)
600 Executive Blvd. Suite 200
Rockville, MD 20852-3801

Panic Assistance League
835 Hopkins Way #211
Redondo Beach, CA 90277

Phobic Update
670 Washington
Braintree, MA 02184

CHAANGE
128 Country Club Drive
Chula Vista, CA 92011

New Horizons
Ed. Carolyn Johnson
101 Village Terrace
Concord, VA 24538

IN CANADA

Free from Fear Foundation Newsletter
1137 Gloucester Square
Pickering, Ontario
LIV 3RI
CANADA

Bridge of Hope Newsletter
Leilani Przada, Editor
P.O. Box 489
Lantzville, BC
VOR 2HO
CANADA

IN ENGLAND

Emotions Self-Help Magazine
Wallsend Self Help Group
P.O. Box 5
Wallsend
Tyne and Wear
England
NE28 6DZ

Please contact these newsletters for subscription information.

Suggested Reading

PANIC DISORDER: What You Don't Know May
Be Dangerous to Your Health*
PANIC DISORDER: The Medical Point of View*
(Revised Edition)
William D. Kernodle, M.D.

The Anxiety Disease *
David Sheehan, M.D.

Don't Panic: Taking Control of Anxiety Attacks *
Breaking the Panic Cycle
Reid Wilson, Ph.D.

Hope and Help for Your Nerves;
Peace from Nervous Suffering;
Simple Effective Treatment of Agoraphobia;
Claire Weekes, M.D.

The Twelve Steps of Phobics Anonymous
Marilyn Gellis, Ph.D. and Rosemary Maut, MA

from Anxiety Addict to Serenity Seeker
Marilyn Gellis, Ph.D.

Triumph Over Fear*
Jerilyn Ross, MA, L.I.C.S.W.

Embracing the Fear
Judy Bemis and Amr Barrada

Anxiety, Phobias, and Panic
Reneau Z. Peurifoy, MA, MFCC

You Have Choices
William N. Penzer, Ph.D. and Bonnie Goodman, MS

The Anxiety and Phobia Workbook
Edmund J. Bourne, Ph.D.

How to Help Your Loved Ones Recover from Agoraphobia
Karen P. Williams

Managing Your Anxiety
Christopher J. McCullough, Ph.D.

Outgrowing Agoraphobia
Christopher J. McCullough, Ph.D.

Freedom from Fears
Ann Seagrove and Faison Covington

The Good News About Panic, Anxiety, and Phobias*
Mark S. Gold, M.D.

Overcoming Panic Attacks: Strategies to Free Yourself From the Anxiety Trap *
S. Babior and C. Goldman

Panic Disorder and Agoraphobia: A Guide *
J.H. Griest and J.W. Jefferson

Mastery of Your Anxiety and Panic *
D.H. Barlow and M.G. Craske

Agoraphobia: Nature and Treatment *
A.M. Mathews; M.G. Gelder; D.W. Johnston

The Complete Agoraphobic Sourcebook
Joan Orrico with Teresa Salas

* Among those included on the resource list of the National Institute of Mental Health. This doesn't imply these are the only valuable books on the subjects of Panic Disorder and Agoraphobia.

About the Editor

Anita Louise Pace grew up in Southern California. She has a Bachelor's Degree in Social Welfare from California State University Northridge. Ms. Pace became disabled from agoraphobia in 1978 and got more serious about writing once she improved enough to do so. She studied screen writing at the Hollywood Scriptwriting Institute and later studied broadcasting. She authored a story in an anthology about women with disabilities, *Living With a Hidden Disability; Agoraphobia,* (With the Power of Each Breath, Cleis Press).

Life Isn't Just a Panic; Stories of Hope by Recovering Agoraphobics is Ms. Pace's third book. The others are *Write from the Heart; Lesbians Healing from Heartache,* and *If You Want to Soar, You've Got to Learn to Fly.*

She lives near Portland, Oregon in a home that includes five dogs and a rabbit. She continues to recover and write when her beasts allow her to.

Contributors

A.B.: "I was born in one of the boroughs of New York City. I was educated there and have a BA in Sociology as well as in Art. I worked briefly for the city and began to paint and photograph about 25 years ago. My subjects are local street scenes, homes, automobiles, trucks, city-scapes, and old storefronts. I have been with many galleries over the years in local areas near the city as well as in Manhattan. I live and paint in my apartment with my cat, KC."

Marie Anderson: "I grew up and still reside in the Los Angeles area. I was the first girl in my family to graduate from high school. I went on to receive my Bachelor of Science degree in Rehabilitation Counseling and Master of Science in Higher Education Counseling. I enjoy reading and spending time with my daughters Janie and Sandi, and grandson, Anthony."

Brenda E. Eads lives on a small farm outside Portland, Indiana, population 6,483. She has been married to an elementary school principal for 24 years and has one daughter. Brenda has had several short stories, articles, and poems published and is working on her second novel. She also enjoys needlework, church activities, and taking care of her poodles. Brenda is on the road to recovery from agoraphobia, and even though it is a very long road, she is delighted to be traveling on it.

Dr. Marilyn Gellis is founder and director of The Institute for Phobic Awareness, Phobics Anonymous World Service Headquarters located in Palm Springs, CA. She's been honored at Palm Springs Continuation School Teacher of the Year for her work with teenage alcohol and drug addicts at a residential recovery facility. Dr. Gellis presently teaches for Charter Behavioral Health

Systems of Southern CA. She has also written two books on the subjects of phobias, anxiety, and panic attacks. She has appeared on numerous radio and on national TV talk shows and is available as a consultant to lecture, conduct workshops, or assist in establishing Phobics Anonymous Chapters.

Jane is 30 years old and loves all animals, especially cats. She enjoys sports: weightlifting, rollerblading, bike riding, golf and most others. She loves the outdoors and skis whenever possible. A goal is to study real estate and she wants to refinish homes for profit. She adds, that she's "on the road to recovery!!"

Gerry Kulpa: "I'm 45 years old live in a log home on seven acres of mostly wooded land in the state of New Jersey. My interests are corresponding with pen pals and writing articles for a local newsletter. I'm currently working on a limited basis for a local video store." Gerry is also an assistant editor for the Panic Relief News.

Rochelle Krupp resides with her husband in Minnesota. She has a son and two stepdaughters. She and her husband own and work a scrap metal business. Rochelle continues to believe there is life after agoraphobia. She finds much joy in her four-legged kids, Buddy and Lucy, her two cocker spaniels.

Carolyn Johnson is a editing a newsletter for panic disorder called *New Horizons*. She had her first p.a.'s in her early 40's and is 59 at time of publication of this book in 1995. Her hobbies include golf, music, and writing.

Molly Matteson was born in the Midwest, but has been a California transplant for 26 years. She likes CA with the possible exception of earthquakes, floods, fires, and riots. Molly loves to write as well as to craft soft-sculpture dolls and paint decorative wood figures. She's "a creative cook (meaning lots of stuff down the disposal)." Molly says she can't live without flowers in her garden. Her best friend is her "hairy dog." Twice married but now single, she has five "adorable" grand-nephews.

Anita L. Pace was born in Los Angeles from where she escaped in late 1990 to Oregon. She is co-mother of five dogs and one rabbit. She wanted to be the first female on the L.A. Dodgers but was relieved to not even be considered when she discovered she'd have to fly. When she isn't being serious or anxious, she enjoys trying to make others laugh. She also enjoys traveling and is awaiting for the bridge to Europe to be constructed.

Susan Jury Park "who has brunette ambition, is single and resides south of the Mason-Dixon line where the streets have no name." Her hobbies include singing, a passion for music, baking pies, listening to audiotapes, playing the flute, photography, and putting Mississsippi on the map! She attended the University of Mississippi and is a member of the World Taekwondo Federation and UM Taekwondo Club with aspirations of someday becoming a black belt.

Ricardo Vicente Reyes is a painter, sculptor, and altar-builder. His work has been featured in books, catalogs, textbooks, and on film. Ricardo was raised in Los Angeles and visited Jalisco, Mexico, as a young man. It was there that he discovered the folk traditions of Southern Mexico. He also found the work of his ancestors-ceramics, textiles, and toys in the museums as well as in homes and personal collections. As a child he was taught by Corita Kent. He has taught secondary students in Los Angeles and San Francisco.

Denise Ranauro lives in Staten Island. Born and raised there, she is married and the mother of two sons. She is a freelance worker in the accounting field. She hopes to return to college to pursue her degree. Her hobby is writing and a goal is to develop the skills to write self-help articles.

Brenda M. Rivet lives in the suburbs of Rhode Island with her husband, Raymond, and son, J.R. "I choose to stay home and take care of my family. My husband and I own a small electronic repair shop which I do the bookkeeping." Her spare time is spent with family, grandchildren, visiting with friends, working in the yard, and on sewing projects. "I still search for answers and enjoy the ones I've found."

Lindsay Sonia lives in her hometown with her mother, stepfather, two brothers, and a sister. "I am employed at the Stop and Shop and am currently struggling to get my G.E.D. I'm taking life day by day, enjoying myself and the family's new addition, my seven month old brother, Brian Robert. A special thanks to my wonderful, loving family and my sister for always running to the store! I love you!"

Rich Sterling lives in the Midwest, enjoys writing, photography, bicycling, and family trips. "I am a volunteer for Cub Scouts, Boy Scouts, and other volunteer programs. I am a former educator working in the business field." Lifetime goals include travel, publishing books to help others with anxiety, and earning my Ph.D. degree.

Jace Ryan Turner "Like most people in this life, I listen too often to the many voices that color my perception of the world, my life. Thus, I find myself lost to what I know, and mixed in a collage to what I feel. And at the age of 21 I realize what a burden these words from the wind carry for my sense of self. So, in short, my life is dedicated to a focus that will provide a clear vision of the path I've traveled and will continue to walk. Bright with love and embraced by arms, my life is a happy one. And when faced by a shortcoming, I simply remember, we're all naked under our clothes."

Johnny Turner is 19 years old and lives with his parents in Santa Barbara.

Susan Turner is a native of California, "perversely proud" that she was born in Hollywood. She's resides in Santa Barbara with her husband and six sons, four of which are canine. Her passions are photography and writing. She ran a support group for four years, works with people dealing with agoraphobia and panic disorder, is a columnist for two newsletters, and is working on an agoraphobia/panic disorder workbook. Although Susan knows better, she adds, "I'm still waiting for that magic "cure" pill (but when invented will be too afraid to swallow.")

Franci Warner has struggled with p.a.'s for 28 years. For four and a half years, until 1995, she published The Mountain Climber newsletter. She has been published 32 times across the country. She has lectured and she sees clients privately in "motivation sessions," as well as running a group every other week.

Other books from Baby Steps Press

Write from the Heart; Lesbians Healing from Heartache

An Anthology

Edited by Anita L. Pace
with questions and answers
by Dakota Sands MSW

This book is filled with stories of recovery by lesbians who have lost their partner by breakup or death. Thousands of women have used Write from the Heart as a tool in their recovery.

"I just finished Write from the Heart. It was the most wonderful think I've ever read."

Omaha, NE

"Your book offers me hope and insight."

Naples, ME

"I now realize healing is possible with time."

Victoria, Australia

"Letting go of 23 years with my beloved partner will never leave me intact, but I shall go through the motions ... knowing others share this pain."

West Palm Beach, FL

If You Want to Soar, You've Got to Learn to Fly

Not just another growing up book. This is a witty, moving account of the author's discovery of self.

"You captured your childhood and all the complexities of growing up, writing it in a wonderful way."
"Be prepared for a treat ... The agony and ecstasy of adolescence are resurrected for the reader ... This is an opportunity for straight Americans to understand the special pains of growing up gay."

Roberta M. Jarrett, author
Caring for the Caregiver
Gifts from the Shore

This book chronicles the life of the author from ages five through twenty in an Italian-Catholic home. With family photos throughout, the reader cannot help but see how much we have in common as people, no matter what our differences.

Order Form

Life Isn't Just a Panic; Stories of Hope by Recovering Agoraphobics

_____ copies at $13.95 each book $ _____

Other Baby Steps Press books:

If You Want to Soar, You've Got to Learn to Fly
            Anita L. Pace

_____ copies at $10.95 each book $ _____

Write from the Heart; Lesbians Healing from Heartache
            edited by Anita L. Pace

_____ copies at $13.95 each book $ _____

    $2.00 shipping and handling for one book $ _____
       .50 each additional book

       Total enclosed* $ _____

Name:_____

Address:_____

City:_____ State:_____ Zip:_____

* All payments in U.S. currency only or International Money Orders.

Please allow 2-4 weeks for delivery. 10% discount for orders of 10 or more books. Books mailed book rate unless otherwise requested. Additional cost for first class.

Send checks to: | **For credit card orders:**
    Baby Steps Press | **Call toll-free**
    P.O. Box 1917   ☎   **Day or night**
    Beaverton, OR 97075   **1-800-444-2524**

Order Form

Life Isn't Just a Panic; Stories of Hope by Recovering Agoraphobics
_____ copies at $13.95 each book $ _____

Other Baby Steps Press books:

**If You Want to Soar, You've Got to Learn to Fly
          Anita L. Pace**
_____ copies at $10.95 each book $ _____

**Write from the Heart; Lesbians Healing from Heartache
          edited by Anita L. Pace**
_____ copies at $13.95 each book $ _____

$2.00 shipping and handling for one book $ _____
    .50 each additional book

    Total enclosed* $ _____

Name:_____

Address:_____

City:_____ State:_____ Zip:_____

* All payments in U.S. currency only or International Money
Orders.

Please allow 2-4 weeks for delivery. 10% discount for orders of 10 or
more books. Books mailed book rate unless otherwise requested.
Additional cost for first class.

Send checks to: | **For credit card orders:**
    Baby Steps Press | **Call toll-free**
    P.O. Box 1917 | **Day or night**
    Beaverton, OR 97075 | **1-800-444-2524**